CITYPACK TOP 25
Istanbul

CHRISTOPHER AND MELANIE RICE
ADDITIONAL WRITING BY TONY KELLY

If you have any comments or suggestions for this guide contact the editor at *Citypack@theAA.com*

AA Publishing
Find out more about AA Publishing and the wide range of services the AA provides by visiting our website at www.theAA.com/travel

How to Use This Book

KEY TO SYMBOLS

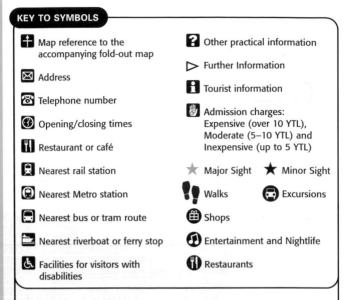

✚ Map reference to the accompanying fold-out map	❓ Other practical information
✉ Address	▷ Further Information
☎ Telephone number	ℹ Tourist information
④ Opening/closing times	✋ Admission charges: Expensive (over 10 YTL), Moderate (5–10 YTL) and Inexpensive (up to 5 YTL)
🍴 Restaurant or café	
🚆 Nearest rail station	★ Major Sight ★ Minor Sight
Ⓜ Nearest Metro station	👣 Walks 🚌 Excursions
🚍 Nearest bus or tram route	🏬 Shops
⛴ Nearest riverboat or ferry stop	🎵 Entertainment and Nightlife
♿ Facilities for visitors with disabilities	🍽 Restaurants

This guide is divided into four sections

• **Essential Istanbul:** An introduction to the city and tips on making the most of your stay.

• **Istanbul by Area:** We've broken the city into five areas, and recommended the best sights, shops, entertainment venues, nightlife and restaurants in each one. Suggested walks help you to explore on foot.

• **Where to Stay:** The best hotels, whether you're looking for luxury, budget or something in between.

• **Need to Know:** The info to make your trip run smoothly, including getting about by public transport, weather tips, emergency phone numbers and useful websites.

Navigation In the Istanbul by Area chapter, we've given each area its own colour, which is also used on the locator maps throughout the book and the map on the inside front cover.

Maps The fold-out map accompanying this book is a comprehensive street plan of Istanbul. The grid on this fold-out map is the same as the grid on the locator maps within the book. We've given grid references within the book for each sight and listing.

Contents

CONTENTS

3

Introducing Istanbul

Istanbul, Byzantium, Constantinople—whatever you call it, this city has always excited the imagination. Once home to two of the world's greatest empires, it straddles the Bosphorus like a bridge between continents, with Europe on one side and Asia on the other.

At first glance, Istanbul is full of contradictions. It's a city of mosques and minarets but it's also the spiritual home of the Orthodox church. It's not even the capital of Turkey—a largely Asian, Muslim country—but could soon be the biggest metropolis in the European Union. Old women in headscarves wander the streets of Fener, while young women in miniskirts stroll along Istiklal Caddesi and drink in trendy bars on their way to the latest opening at Istanbul Modern. It may be a cliché, but Istanbul seems torn between ancient and modern, east and west.

Look more closely and you see a confident, forward-looking city, which is rediscovering its Ottoman heritage at the same time as embracing Europe. In music, art, fashion and cuisine, young Turks are seeking inspiration in the past to create a 21st-century Ottoman chic. Most visitors are attracted by the beauty of the Blue Mosque, but the legacy of the Ottoman empire is more than just a collection of monuments.

At the junction of the Golden Horn and the Bosphorus, Istanbul is a city on the water. Stand on the dockside at Eminönü, beneath the Galata Bridge, at dusk. The scent of grilled mackerel mingles with the soundtrack of city life, as taxi horns, honking ferries and Arabesque music almost drown out the call to prayer from a thousand minarets. As the sun sets over the water and the domes of Istanbul are silhouetted against the sky, it is impossible not to be seduced by this unique city.

Facts + Figures

Population: 10–15 million
Growth rate: 1,000 per day
Annual visitors: 5 million
Mobile phone use: 85 per cent
Mosques: 2,500

BRIDGING THE GAP

The 1.5km (1 mile) Bosphorus suspension bridge, opened in 1973 between Beylerbeyi and Ortaköy, carries more than 180,000 vehicles between Europe and Asia each day. At one time, pedestrians were allowed to walk across, but this is no longer permitted due to the high number of suicide attempts.

THE MAKER OF ISTANBUL

If one man has had the greatest impact on the appearance of present-day Istanbul, it is probably Mimar Sinan (1490–1588), who was chief imperial architect under Sultan Süleyman the Magnificent at the height of the Ottoman empire. His legacy includes the Çemberlitaş baths, Rüstem Paşa Mosque and Süleymaniye Mosque.

SOUNDS OF THE CITY

Fatih Akın's film *Crossing the Bridge: The Sound of Istanbul* (2005) explored Istanbul's music scene, bringing artists such as Kurdish singer Aynur, Gypsy clarinettist Selim Sesler, Sufi DJ Mercan Dede and psychedelic folk rockers Baba Zula to a global audience—two years after Turkish pop star Sertab Erener won the Eurovision Song Contest.

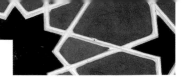

A Short Stay in Istanbul

DAY 1

Morning Explore the main sights of Sultanahmet. The best place to get your bearings is **At Meydanı** (the Hippodrome, ▷ 25), which is well placed for visiting the **Sultanahmet Camii** (Blue Mosque, ▷ 32).

Mid-morning Enjoy a Turkish tea or coffee at **Derviş** (▷ 43), opposite the Blue Mosque, then cross the park to **Ayasofya Camii** (▷ 26) to admire the mosaics of this magnificent Byzantine church. Afterwards, you can visit **Yerebatan Sarnıcı** (▷ 37), a vast, atmospheric underground cathedral of water.

Lunch There are several lunchtime options near the foot of **Divan Yolu** (▷ 38), but for an inexpensive, classic Turkish snack, try the *köfte* (meatballs) at **Tarihi Sultanahmet Köftecisi** (▷ 44).

Afternoon Walk or take the tram up Divan Yolu to **Beyazıt**, then spend a couple of hours shopping in the **Kapalı Çarşı** (Grand Bazaar, ▷ 50). All that bargaining can be exhausting, so treat yourself to a soothing steam bath and massage at **Çemberlitaş Hamamı** (▷ 49), a beautiful Turkish bath designed by Mimar Sinan.

Early evening Take the tram to Eminönü and hop on a ferry to **Üsküdar** (▷ 101), then stroll along the waterfront to **Kız Kulesi** (▷ 100) to admire the views.

Dinner Stay in Üsküdar for dinner at **Kanaat** (▷ 106), a historic *lokanta* and Istanbul institution. Alternatively, take the ferry back to Eminönü and cross the road to **Hamdi Et Lokantası** (▷ 62).

Evening Relax with a drink at a café beneath **Galata Bridge** (▷ 56).

DAY 2

Morning Arrive at the Topkapı Sarayı (Topkapı Palace, ▷ 34) at 9am, when the gates open, and allow a whole morning for your visit. It's impossible to see everything in one visit, so concentrate on the Treasury, imperial costumes, collection of arms and the relics of the Prophet Muhammad. Take the guided tour of the Harem for a fascinating insight into the lives of the sultans and the Ottoman court.

Lunch Konyalı (▷ 44), in the palace gardens, is a popular spot for lunch, so get there early for a table on the terrace, with views over the Bosphorus.

Afternoon Stroll through the grounds of Topkapı Palace to **Gülhane Parkı** (▷ 39), with its views of the Bosphorus, then take the tram across Galata Bridge to **Tophane** (▷ 84). For a complete contrast to Topkapı, visit **Istanbul Modern** (▷ 78).

Early evening Continue on the tram to Kabataş, then transfer to the funicular for the short ascent to **Taksim Meydanı** (▷ 84). From here, you can join the early-evening promenade along **Istiklal Caddesi** (▷ 80).

Dinner Enjoy a feast of *mezes* washed down with *rakı* at one of the *meyhanes* along **Nevizade Sokağı** (▷ 88–89) or **Çiçek Pasajı** (▷ 82).

Evening Stay in Beyoğlu to catch some live music at the bars and clubs off Istiklal Caddesi. Depending on your taste, you could hear jazz at **Nardis** (▷ 87), rock at **Babylon** (▷ 86), Anatolian *saz* at **Munzur** (▷ 87), or take in a classical performance at **Atatürk Cultural Centre** (▷ 86).

Top 25

ESSENTIAL ISTANBUL TOP 25

8

These pages are a quick guide to the Top 25, which are described in more detail later. Here they are listed alphabetically. The tinted background shows the area they are in.

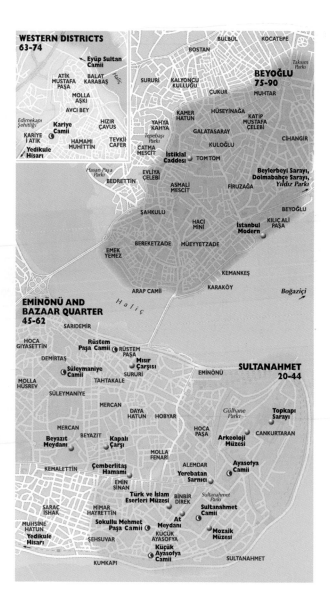

WESTERN DISTRICTS
63–74

Eyüp Sultan Camii

ATİK MUSTAFA PAŞA   BALAT KARABAŞ

MOLLA AŞKI

AVCI BEY

Edirnekapı Şehitliği   Kariye Camii   HIZIR ÇAVUŞ

KARİYE İ ATİK   HAMAMI MUHİTTİN   TEVKİİ CAFER

Yedikule Hisarı

Hasan Paşa Parkı   BEDRETTİN

BÜLBÜL   KOCATEPE

BOSTAN

Taksım Parkı

SURURİ   KALYONCU KULLUĞU

ÇUKUR

BEYOĞLU
75–90

MUHTAR

KAMER HATUN   HÜSEYİNAĞA   KATİP MUSTAFA ÇELEBİ

YAHYA KAHYA   GALATASARAY

Tepebaşı Parkı   KULOĞLU   CİHANGİR

ÇATMA MESCİT   İstiklal Caddesi   TOMTOM

EVLİYA ÇELEBİ   Beylerbeyi Sarayı, Dolmabahçe Sarayı, Yıldız Parkı

ASMALI MESCİT   FİRUZAĞA

ŞAHKULU   BEYOĞLU

HACI MİNİ   İstanbul Modern   KILIÇ ALİ PAŞA

BEREKETZADE   MÜEYYETZADE

EMEK YEMEZ

KEMANKEŞ

ARAP CAMİİ   KARAKÖY   Boğaziçi

EMİNÖNÜ AND
BAZAAR QUARTER
45–62

Haliç

SARIDEMİR

HOCA GIYASETTİN   Rüstem Paşa Camii   RÜSTEM PAŞA

DEMİRTAŞ   Mısır Çarşısı

Süleymaniye Camii   SURURİ   EMİNÖNÜ

MOLLA HÜSREV   TAHTAKALE

SÜLEYMANİYE

MERCAN   DAYA HATUN   HOBYAR

Gülhane Parkı   Topkapı Sarayı

MERCAN   HOCA PAŞA   CANKURTARAN

Beyazıt Meydanı   BEYAZIT   Kapalı Çarşı   Arkeoloji Müzesi

MOLLA FENARİ

KEMALETTİN   Çemberlitaş Hamamı   ALEMDAR   Ayasofya Camii

EMİN SİNAN   Yerebatan Sarnıcı

SULTANAHMET
20–44

Türk ve İslam Eserleri Müzesi   BİNBİR DİREK   Sultanahmet Parkı

SARAÇ İSHAK   MİMAR HAYRETTİN   Sultanahmet Camii

MUHSİNE HATUN   Sokullu Mehmet Paşa Camii   At Meydanı

Yedikule Hisarı   ŞEHSUVAR   KÜÇÜK AYASOFYA   Mozaik Müzesi

Küçük Ayasofya Camii

KUMKAPI   SULTANAHMET

Shopping

Istanbul provides retail therapy for even the most jaded shopper. Few people leave without a souvenir, whether it's a handwoven Turkish carpet or a box of *lokum* (Turkish delight).

The Bazaars

The ultimate shopping experience is the Grand Bazaar (▷ 50–51), in business since the Ottoman conquest. Entire streets are dedicated to jewellery, leather and clothes. Among the items on sale are carpets, kilims (flat-woven rugs), ceramic tiles, gold and silver, meerschaum pipes, silk and cotton clothing, backgammon and chess sets, jewellery boxes, belly-dancing costumes and *nargiles* (water pipes, ▷ panel, 86).

Shopping in the bazaar is great fun but it has become something of a game, with pushy traders enticing you into their shops and potential customers attempting to resist their charms. Most of what is on sale in the bazaar these days is aimed at tourists, and most locals prefer to shop in the Tahtakale district, between the Grand and Spice bazaars. The streets here are always crowded with shoppers searching for inexpensive clothes.

Meanwhile, if you want to buy a carpet but find the Grand Bazaar intimidating, the Arasta Bazaar, beside the Blue Mosque, has a row of smart shops in a former stable turned shopping arcade, offering high-quality

---

THE EVIL EYE

A popular souvenir is a *nazar bonjuk*, a good-luck charm supposed to protect the wearer against the 'evil eye'. Made out of blown glass with a blue 'eye' at the middle, these are sold all over Istanbul as bracelets, earrings and pins. They are based on a superstition that one person can cast a spell on another simply by looking at them. No one really believes this any more, but many people still wear a *nazar bonjuk* just in case.

Souvenirs range from traditional Turkish dolls and water pipes to brightly embroidered slippers

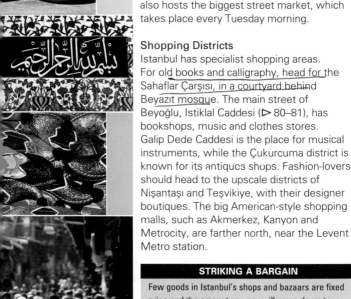

carpets, rugs, jewellery and ceramics. You may pay a little bit more, but the experience is more relaxed.

Herbs and spices, dried fruits, scented teas and Turkish delight can all be found in the Spice Bazaar (▷ 52). There are excellent specialist food shops and delicatessens on and around Güneşlibahçe Sokağı, a short walk from the ferry terminal in Kadıköy. Come here for bread, cheese, sausages, yogurt, olives, olive oil and honey. Kadıköy also hosts the biggest street market, which takes place every Tuesday morning.

Shopping Districts

Istanbul has specialist shopping areas. For old books and calligraphy, head for the Sahaflar Çarşısı, in a courtyard behind Beyazıt mosque. The main street of Beyoğlu, Istiklal Caddesi (▷ 80–81), has bookshops, music and clothes stores. Galip Dede Caddesi is the place for musical instruments, while the Çukurcuma district is known for its antiques shops. Fashion-lovers should head to the upscale districts of Nişantaşı and Teşvikiye, with their designer boutiques. The big American-style shopping malls, such as Akmerkez, Kanyon and Metrocity, are farther north, near the Levent Metro station.

STRIKING A BARGAIN

Few goods in Istanbul's shops and bazaars are fixed price and the amount you pay will come down to bargaining. Many visitors find this custom irritating, but stay polite and good-natured and it is all part of the fun. The shopkeeper will start at a price well above what he is prepared to accept; the customer will offer much less and eventually they will meet in the middle. With major purchases such as a carpet, the process can be drawn out over endless cups of tea. In the end, remember that what matters is not whether you pay the lowest price but that you buy something you like at a price that you are happy with.

Shopping by Theme

Whether you want to hunt for bargains in bazaars or seek out the latest fashions in designer boutiques, you'll find it all in Istanbul. On this page shops are listed by theme. For more detailed information, see the listings in Istanbul by Area.

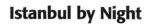

Istanbul by Night

If most visitors to Istanbul spend their days in Sultanahmet exploring museums, mosques and bazaars, then Beyoğlu, on the far side of the Galata Bridge, is definitely the place to go after dark.

Plenty of Choice

On summer evenings, Istiklal Caddesi resembles an endless fashion parade and music pours out of countless bars. From intimate jazz clubs and live folk music venues to rowdy *meyhanes* where gypsy musicians tour the tables while the customers knock back the *rakı*, you are bound to find something that appeals.

Summer by the Sea

In summer, the clubbing crowd moves down to the Bosphorus, to open-air mega-clubs in Ortaköy and Kuruçeşme, either side of the Bosphorus Bridge. If you prefer caffeine to alcohol, head for one of the many *çay bahçesi* (tea gardens) to sip coffee.

Night Light

Sultanahmet is mostly quiet after dark, apart from the backpacker bars along Akbıyık Caddesi. However, the Blue Mosque is brilliantly illuminated at night and there are few experiences to beat sitting on a terrace with a view of the Blue Mosque as the call to prayer drifts across the city.

AN EVENING STROLL

Take the ferry from Sirkeci to Harem on the Asian shore. Behind the landing stage are the Selimiye barracks, where British nurse Florence Nightingale set up her hospital during the Crimean War. Walk north-wards along the waterfront promenade, with views of the Topkapı Palace, Ayasofya and Blue Mosque. On an island at the entrance to the Bosphorus, the 18th-century Kız Kulesi (Maiden's Tower, ▷ 100) comes into view. Continue walking to reach Üsküdar, where you can catch a ferry back to Eminönü.

Watch some dancing, browse a night market or enjoy a meal alfresco

Eating Out

From barbecued fish on the quayside at Eminönü to romantic restaurants serving new-wave fusion cuisine, Istanbul offers a full range of dining experiences.

What to Eat
Gone are the days when eating out in Turkey meant a *döner kebap* from a street stall. You will still find these all over the city, but even the humble *kebap* now comes in a variety of options. Traditional Turkish cooking is based on fresh local ingredients, especially lamb, fish and vegetables, while 'modern Turkish' cuisine blends Turkish and global influences.

Where to Eat
A *restoran* is a formal restaurant, while a *lokanta* is more casual, serving ready-prepared meals and grilled meat, but usually no alcohol. *Meyhanes* (▷ 88) are taverns offering tapas-like *mezes* to share, while *pide salonu* specialize in *pide*, a pizza-type flatbread. For fresh fish, head for Kumkapı (▷ 44) or the villages beside the Bosphorus.

Practicalities
Most restaurants open from around noon to midnight. Smoking is ubiquitous. Tipping is expected; it is usual to add 10 per cent.

TASTY TURKISH DISHES
Arnavut ciğeri—spicy liver with onions
Çerkez tavuğu—chicken in walnut purée
Döner kebap—lamb grilled on a spit
İç pilav—rice with nuts, currants and onions
İmam bayıldı—aubergines (eggplants) with tomatoes and onions
Mantı—ravioli with yoghurt
Piyaz—haricot bean salad
Sigara böreği—fried filo pastry filled with cheese
Şiş köfte—grilled meatballs
Su böreği—baked pastry filled with meat or cheese
Tas kebap—vegetable and meat stew
Yaprak dolma—stuffed vine leaves

If you're in a hurry, try a take-away kebab, a snack from a street stand or a pastry or delicious dessert

Restaurants by Cuisine

Istanbul has restaurants to suit all tastes and budgets. On this page they are listed by cuisine. For more detailed descriptions, see the individual listings in Istanbul by Area.

ASIAN

Banyan (▷ 105)

FISH AND SEAFOOD

Ali Baba (▷ 105)
Aquarius (▷ 105)
Asmalımescit Balıkçısı (▷ 88)
Baba (▷ 105)
Beyaz (▷ 44)
Ceneviz Café (▷ 105)
Çinar (▷ 105)
Deniz Kızı (▷ 106)
Kavak Doğanay (▷ 106)
Rumeli Iskele (▷ 106)
Yelken (▷ 106)
Yoros Café (▷ 106)

FRENCH

Café du Levant (▷ 74)

FUSION/TRENDY

Lokanta (▷ 88)
Mikla (▷ 90)
Vogue (▷ 106)

MEDITERRANEAN

Amedros (▷ 44)
Halat (▷ 74)
Rumeli Café (▷ 44)

RUSSIAN

Galata Evi (▷ 88)

SPANISH

Venta del Toro (▷ 90)

SWEETS

Asırlık Kanlıca Yoğurdu (▷ 105)
Mado (▷ 88)
Patisserie Markiz (▷ 90)

TURKISH: ANATOLIAN

Otantik (▷ 90)

TURKISH: ELEGANT

Clement's (▷ 105)
Körfez (▷ 106)

TURKISH: GRILLED MEAT

Aya Yorgi Manastiri (▷ 105)
Develi (▷ 74)
Doy-Doy (▷ 44)
Hamdi Et Lokantası (▷ 62)
Tarihi Sultanahmet Köftecisi (▷ 44)

TURKISH: LOKANTA

Hacı Abdullah (▷ 88)
Kanaat (▷ 106)

TURKISH: MEYHANE

Boncuk (▷ 88)
Imroz (▷ 88)
Neyle Meyle (▷ 90)
Palmiye (▷ 90)
Refik (▷ 90)
Sofyalı 9 (▷ 90)

TURKISH: SNACKS

Kariye Pembe Köşk (▷ 74)

TURKISH: TRADITIONAL

Asitane (▷ 74)
Darüzziyafe (▷ 62)
Konyalı (▷ 44)
Pandeli (▷ 62)
Rami (▷ 44)
Sarniç (▷ 44)

VEGETARIAN

Nature & Peace (▷ 90)

If You Like...

However you'd like to spend your time in Istanbul, these top suggestions should help you tailor your ideal visit. Each sight or listing has a fuller write-up in Istanbul by Area.

CATCHING LOCAL MUSIC

Join a lively late-night crowd to hear Anatolian folk musicians at Munzur (▷ 87).
See the whirling dervishes at Galata Mevlevihanesi (▷ 86).
Spend an evening at Kumkapı (▷ panel, 44), being serenaded by gypsy *fasıl* musicians.

ISLAMIC ART AND ARCHITECTURE

Marvel at the Iznik tiles at the exquisite Rüstem Paşa Mosque (▷ 53).
Visit Sokullu Mehmet Paşa Mosque (▷ 30), one of Mimar Sinan's finest creations.
Explore the history of Islamic art at the Museum of Turkish and Islamic Art (▷ 36).
Relax in a historic Turkish bath at Çemberlitaş Hamamı (▷ 49).

Inside Sokullu Mehmet Paşa Mosque (above); whirling dervishes (top)

WATERSIDE DINING

Enjoy fresh fish beside the Bosphorus in the garden at Yelken (▷ 106).
Take the ferry to Anadolu Kavağı for lunch at Baba (▷ 105).
Take your pick of the many restaurants beneath Galata Bridge (▷ 56).

OTTOMAN CHIC

Taste new versions of classic Ottoman dishes at Asitane (▷ 74).
Stay in a restored Ottoman house, such as Empress Zoe hotel (▷ 110).
Buy shirts and bath towels inspired by Ottoman designs at Derviş (▷ 59).

A yacht passes the hilltop castle at Anadolu Kavağı (above right); experience some Ottoman chic at Empress Zoe hotel (right)

Souvenir shopping (right); the Eyüp Ensari mausoleum (below)

BARGAIN-HUNTING

Browse the antiques shops of Çukurcuma (▷ 82).
Visit Ortaköy (▷ 101) on Sunday morning, when artists sell their work in the street.
Go prepared to haggle for everything from Turkish carpets to chess sets in the Grand Bazaar (▷ 50).
Pick up Turkish CDs at bargain prices in the shops on Istiklal Caddesi (▷ 80).

MEETING THE LOCALS

Check out the food shops and delicatessens at Kadıköy (▷ 100).
Make the pilgrimage to Eyüp (▷ 66) on Sunday morning.
Join the early-evening promenade along Istiklal Caddesi (▷ 80).
Drink tea and play backgammon in a traditional Turkish café like Yeni Marmara (▷ 43).

GETTING AWAY FROM IT ALL

Leave the city behind by taking the boat to the Princes' Islands in summer (▷ 102).
Take a picnic to Yıldız Park (▷ 98).
Stroll through Gülhane Park (▷ 39) for tea overlooking the Bosphorus at Set Üstü (▷ 43).
Cruise the Bosphorus (▷ 95).

Across the Bosphorus (above)

SLEEPING IN STYLE

Live the high life in a wooden mansion at Les Ottomans (▷ 112).
Sleep like a sultan at the Çirağan Palace Hotel (▷ 112).
Follow in Agatha Christie's footsteps at the Pera Palas (▷ 84).

The Çirağan Palace at Beşiktaş is now a luxury hotel (left)

BIRD'S-EYE VIEWS

View from the top of the Galata Tower

Ride the cable car to the Pierre Loti Café (▷ 66), overlooking the Golden Horn.

Visit the observation platform at the top of Galata Tower (▷ 82–83).

Climb to the ruined castle above Anadolu Kavağı (▷ 99) for views of the Bosphorus and Black Sea.

Take a taxi to Büyük Çamlıca (▷ 99) to gaze over the city.

SAMPLING LOCAL FOOD

Feast on delicious *mezes* and *pide* bread at Develi (▷ 74).

Tuck into the house special at Haci Abdullah (▷ 00), the best of Istanbul's *lokantas*.

Enjoy grilled mackerel from the night barbecues at Eminönü (▷ panel, 62).

SOMETHING FOR NOTHING

Take advantage of free admission on Thursdays at Istanbul Modern (▷ 78).

Visit the Blue Mosque (▷ 32)—entry to mosques is free but a donation is appreciated.

Soak up the atmosphere of the carpet auction on Wednesday in the Grand Bazaar (▷ 50).

Take the ferry along the Golden Horn (▷ 71) not quite free but worth it for the views alone.

Locally caught fish; the Blue Mosque (above)

KEEPING THE KIDS HAPPY

Walk through a miniature version of Turkey at Miniatürk (▷ 72).

Relive your childhood at Istanbul Toy Museum (▷ 100).

Gorge on free samples of Turkish delight at the Spice Bazaar (▷ 52).

Don't leave Istanbul without trying some Turkish delight (right)

Istanbul by Area

Sultanahmet is the heart of old Istanbul. The Blue Mosque, Ayasofya and Topkapı Palace are all here, along with several interesting museums.

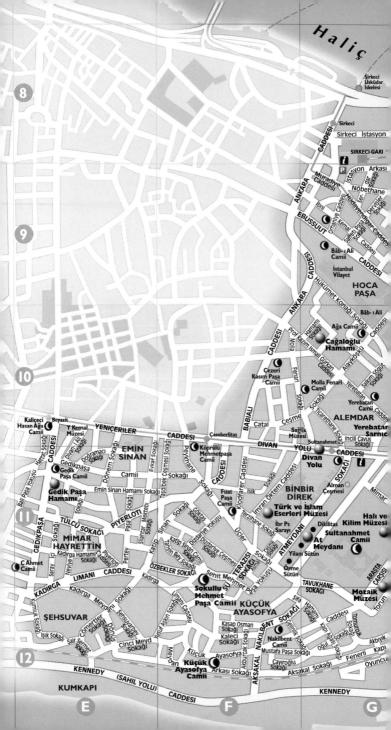

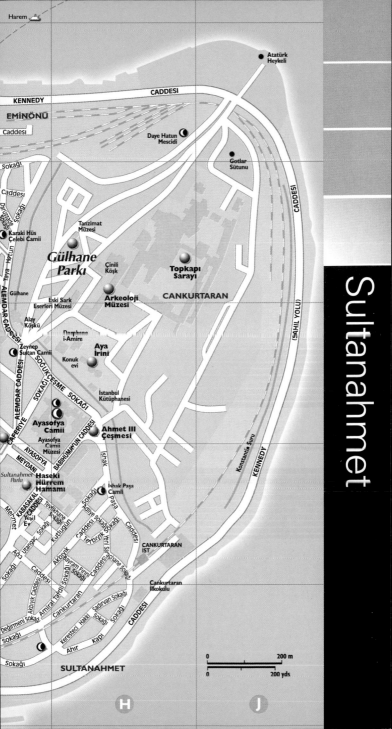

Arkeoloji Müzesi

The Archaeological Museum contains some wonderful sculptures

THE BASICS

✚ H9
✉ Osman Hamdi Bey Yokuşu, Gülhane Parkı
☎ 212-520-7740
🕓 Tue–Sun 9–5
🍴 Garden café (€)
🚇 Gülhane
♿ Few
💲 Inexpensive

HIGHLIGHTS

● Alexander sarcophagus
● Sarcophagus of the Mourning Women
● Lycian Sarcophagus
● Statue of Oceanus
● Bust of Emperor Augustus
● Phrygian alabaster perfume bottle in the shape of a goddess
● Gold earrings from Bronze Age Troy
● 5th-century BC statue of wild boar from Edirne
● 1st-century BC sundial from Mesopotamia
● Treaty of Kadesh
● Tiled Kiosk of Sultan Mehmet the Conqueror

The Archaeological Museum's collections span 5,000 years. The star attraction is the Alexander sarcophagus, adorned with hunting and battle scenes of astonishing intensity.

Archaeological Museum Built to house the sarcophagi of the ancient Phoenician kings recovered by the archaeologist Osman Hamdi Bey in 1887, the museum also boasts a superb collection of classical sculptures. They include astonishingly lifelike busts of the Roman emperors, funerary stelae and a number of well-preserved statues. The new wing hosts a fascinating exhibition on the history of the area. Here you will find fragments of artwork preserved from lost Byzantine churches and a section of the defensive chain that hung across the Golden Horn in the 15th century.

Museum of the Ancient Orient Two 14th-century BC Hittite stone lions guard the entrance to this separate museum, which houses the oldest objects in the collection, including the 6th-century BC glazed-tile reliefs that lined the Processional Way into Babylon. There is a fabulous collection of cuneiform tablets—including the world's oldest peace accord, the Treaty of Kadesh, signed in the 13th century BC—together with law codes, judgements on murder and possibly the world's oldest love poem. The nearby Çinili Köşk (Tiled Pavilion) was built for Sultan Mehmet the Conqueror and is now a museum of ceramics from all over Turkey.

The Egyptian Obelisk
(left and middle);
the Kaiser Wilhelm
fountain (right)

At Meydanı

The most remarkable item in the Hippodrome is the Egyptian Obelisk, dating back to the 16th century BC. The hieroglyphs are so sharply etched that the column looks like a reproduction.

At Meydanı Originally a racecourse for charioteers, the Hippodrome was laid out on the site of the present park by the Emperor Septimius Severus in AD203 and enlarged by Constantine in the 4th century. The leading chariot teams, the Blues and the Greens, evolved into political factions and, in AD532, rioted against the Emperor Justinian, provoking General Belisarius to storm the Hippodrome, with the loss of 30,000 lives. The amphitheatre, which could hold 100,000 people, was destroyed during the Fourth Crusade and the Ottomans plundered the ruins for the Sultanahmet Mosque. From the 16th century the square was known as At Meydanı (Horses' Square), after a polo-like game played here by the sultan's pages.

Monuments on the *spina* The racetrack was divided by a raised platform (*spina*), crowded with statues and monuments. Three of these survive, albeit in truncated form: the Egyptian Obelisk, commissioned by Pharaoh Thutmose III in the 16th century BC and brought to the city by Emperor Theodosius in AD390; the Serpent Column, imported by Constantine from the Temple of Apollo in Delphi (commemorating a 479BC victory over the Persians); and the 10th-century Column of Constantine Porphyrogenitus.

THE BASICS

- ✚ G11
- ✉ At Meydanı, Sultanahmet
- 🍴 Cafés around the edge (€)
- 🚊 Sultanahmet
- ♿ None
- 🎟 Free

HIGHLIGHTS

- ● Kaiser Wilhelm fountain
- ● Egyptian Obelisk
- ● Serpent Column
- ● Column of Constantine Porphyrogenitus
- ● Brick and stone façade of Ibrahim Paşa Sarayı (Museum of Turkish and Islamic Art, ▷ 36)
- ● Milion Taşı (First Milestone)
- ● View of Sultanahmet Mosque

Haghia Sophia – closed mondays

Ayasofya Camii

TOP **25**

HIGHLIGHTS

- Viking graffiti
- Gold mosaic ceiling in vestibule
- Shafts of light through 40 windows of dome
- Carved capitals
- Tinted marbles
- The Virgin and Christ flanked by Justinian and Constantine (mosaic in vestibule)
- Deisis mosaic in gallery
- 'Weeping column'

Despite the peeling mosaics and crumbling masonry, this remains one of the world's architectural masterpieces. Insert your finger into the 'weeping column' in the nave—it is said to have miraculous healing powers.

History Ayasofya (or Haghia Sophia), the Church of Divine Wisdom, was commissioned by the Emperor Justinian in AD532. Despite its immense size—for a long time this was the largest religious building in the world—Ayasofya was completed in five years. Earthquakes nearly destroyed the building shortly afterwards, but despite this it remained the most important church in Christendom for nearly a thousand years. When Constantinople fell to the Turks in 1453, Sultan Mehmet II

Clockwise from left: marble pillars and ornate decoration inside Ayasofya Camii; the Deisis mosaic shows Christ flanked by John the Baptist and the Virgin Mary; the striking exterior; a vivid ceiling mosaic; an intricately carved capital; a mosaic showing the Virgin and Child

decreed the basilica should become a mosque. Since 1934 it has been the Ayasofya Museum.

Mosaics The walls and pillars of the basilica are patterned and decorated marble, brought from all over the known world: white marble from Marmara, purple porphyry from Egypt, verd antique from Thessaly and yellow marble from North Africa. But the chief glory of Ayasofya is its mosaics. There were originally more than 1.6ha (4 acres) of gold tesserae, and although a great deal has since disappeared you can still see some superb figurative mosaics, from the 9th to 13th centuries, in the Vestibule of the Warriors (narthex) and the galleries. There are portraits of emperors and an incomplete but arresting Deisis (Christ flanked by the Virgin Mary and John the Baptist).

THE BASICS

✚ H10
✉ Ayasofya Meydanı, Sultanahmet
☎ 212-522-0989
◷ Summer Tue–Sun 9–7.30; winter Tue–Sun 9–5
🍴 Cafés (€), restaurants (€€) nearby
🚇 Sultanahmet
♿ None
🖐 Moderate
❓ Additional charge for photography

Küçük Ayasofya Camii

TOP 25

The mosque began life as a 6th-century church, commissioned by Emperor Justinian

THE BASICS

➕ F12
✉ Küçük Ayasofya Caddesi
🕐 Hours of prayer
♿ None
💰 Free/donation

HIGHLIGHTS

● Carved capitals on pillars
● Monogram of Justinian and Theodora on pillar
● Frieze celebrating Justinian, Theodora and Sergius (under gallery)
● Remains of 6th-century marble facings
● Irregular octagonal nave
● First-floor gallery

TIP

● Spend time relaxing in the charming courtyard, whose 16th-century *medrese* cells now house tea gardens, booksellers and artists' studios.

This pearl of a church, almost certainly the oldest in Istanbul, has an unusual octagonal design that has sometimes been put down to hurried workmanship but which adds to the building's charm.

Christian beginnings The 'Little' Ayasofya Mosque is even older than the great Byzantine church it resembles. It was commissioned by the Emperor Justinian in about AD527 from the architect Anthemius of Tralles, who also worked on Ayasofya. It was converted to a mosque early in the 16th century by the head of the Black Eunuchs, Hüseyin Ağa, who is buried in a tomb north of the apse. Damaged by earthquakes in 1648 and 1763, the mosque has now been restored to its former glory by the World Monuments Fund.

SS Sergius and Bacchus Emperor Justinian chose two martyred Roman soldiers, Sergius and Bacchus, to be patrons for his church. As a young man Justinian was accused of treason; it is said that Sergius and Bacchus had saved his life by appearing in a dream to the Emperor Anastasius and proclaiming his innocence.

A Byzantine survivor You'll find plenty of evidence of the mosque's earlier history, from the intricately carved decoration on the column capitals, some of which bear Justinian's monogram, to the traces of original gold leaf and marble that once adorned the church.

Mozaik Müzesi

One of the many remnants on view in the Mosaic Museum shows an elephant strangling a lion with its trunk—a scene that may have been acted out in the Belgrade Forest 15 centuries ago.

The palace The mosaics were discovered during excavations in the Arasta Bazaar in the 1930s and '50s. They are thought to date from the 6th century AD and to belong to the first imperial palace, begun in the reign of Constantine (AD324–37), which eventually stretched all the way from the Hippodrome to the sea walls.

The museum Little of the palace remains today apart from the ruined loggia at the entrance to the port and the superb mosaic friezes and pavements. These belonged to the peristyle (colonnade) of the Great Palace and would have been seen by the emperors when they retired to their private apartments. The cubes of glass, stone and terracotta radiate hues, while the action-packed scenes open a fascinating window onto everyday life in Byzantium. In one, a man falls from a donkey loaded with fruit; in another, a bear devours a young stag. There is a predilection for animal hunts, but there are more domestic scenes too: birds perching in a cypress tree, or two children riding on a camel. The most splendid image is of Dionysus, the Greek god of wine and fruitfulness, his luxuriant beard wreathed in green acanthus leaves.

THE BASICS

✚ G11

✉ Torun Sokağı, Sultanahmet

☎ 212-518-1205

🕐 Tue–Sun 9–4.30

🍴 Cafés (€) and restaurants (€€) nearby

♿ None

💷 Inexpensive

❓ The marble window frames of the original palace can be seen on the seafront at Kennedy Caddesi

HIGHLIGHTS

● Mosaic fragments in Arasta Bazaar
● Mosaics: man falling from donkey; camel ride; Dionysus tiger hunt; bear and stag; fight between an elephant and a lion

TIP

● To see more remains of Constantine's Great Palace, visit the museum at Eresin Crown hotel (▷ 112).

Sokullu Mehmet Paşa Camii

HIGHLIGHTS

- Tiled cap of *mimbar*
- Tiles on mihrab wall
- Pointed arches in courtyard
- Fragments from the Kaaba
- Lozenge capitals
- Arabesque paintings under gallery
- Ablution fountain
- Faïence panels above windows and doors

Istanbul's mosques are schools of religion as well as places of worship. In the courtyard of Sokullu Paşa you may hear the rhythmic hum of boys reciting the Koran, as they have done for centuries.

Sokullu Paşa This small masterpiece by Mimar Sinan was commissioned by the Sultan's grand vizier, Sokullu Mehmet Paşa, in 1571–72. Born in Višegrad, Bosnia, in 1505, this formidable politician rose from falconer to viceroy of Europe before being appointed chief minister in 1565. His skills as a naval commander recommended him to Süleyman's successors and he achieved a notable victory in the capture of Tunis in 1574. Sokullu Paşa dedicated the mosque that bears his name to his wife, Ismihan Sultan, daughter of Selim II.

The Sokullu Mehmet Paşa Mosque, with its stunning tile decoration, dates from the 16th century

Interior The prayer hall of this well-proportioned building is a model of taste and refinement. Sinan planned it as a hexagon within a rectangle, the unusually high dome supported at the corners by four smaller semi-domes. A low gallery around three sides of the hall rests on slender marble columns with characteristic Ottoman lozenge capitals. The chief glory of the mosque is the mihrab wall, stunningly arrayed in tiles from the Iznik workshops. Swirling patterns of green and red tulips and carnations on a turquoise ground thrive in a visual context of pure white stone. Other treasures include some original painted arabesques under the gallery, fragments of black stone from the Kaaba in Mecca (above the entrance and in the mihrab wall) and the tiled crown on the *mimbar*, the only one of its kind in Istanbul.

THE BASICS

⊞ F11

✉ Şehit Mehmet Paşa Sokak

🕐 Hours of prayer

♿ None

💰 Free/donation

TIP

● If the mosque is closed, you can usually find a guardian to show you around in exchange for a donation.

Sultanahmet Camii

Better known to Western visitors as the 'Blue Mosque' because of the cobalt tiles in the prayer hall, this awesome building is particularly impressive when illuminated at night.

New mosque When Sultan Ahmet proposed building a new mosque in 1609, his advisers begged him to think again as the treasury was empty after a succession of failed military campaigns. But the sultan would have none of it and even insisted on digging the foundations himself. Sedefkar Mehmet Ağa, a pupil of Mimar Sinan, designed the mosque, which was completed in 1616. It immediately became the focus of religious activities in the city—every Friday the sultan's procession would make its way from Topkapı Palace.

The Blue Mosque is an Istanbul landmark

Külliye The inner courtyard comprises an ornamental fountain and a beautifully proportioned portico of 26 porphyry columns surmounted by 30 domes, while the view from above is of domes and semi-domes cascading from the mosque's summit in an apparently unbroken sequence.

Interior Inside, more than 20,000 Iznik tiles decorate the walls and galleries. Delicately painted with floral and geometrical designs, they are the work of a master craftsman, Çinici Hasan Usta. The stencils around the dome and the pillars are comparatively modern. Take a close look at the wooden doors and window frames, with their inlay of ivory, tortoiseshell and mother-of-pearl, and at the beautiful carving on the *mimbar* and the sultan's loge.

THE BASICS

➕ G11
🗺 Sultanahmet Meydanı, Sultanahmet
☎ 212-518-1319
🕐 Daily; closed to visitors at prayer times, including Friday 11.45– 2.15
🍽 Cafés (€) and restaurants (€€) nearby
🚇 Sultanahmet
♿ None
💷 Free/donation

33

Closed Tuesdays.

Topkapı Sarayı

TOP 25

Palace

HIGHLIGHTS

- Baghdad Pavilion
- Circumcision Room
- Divan
- Harem
- Relics of the Prophet Muhammad
- Sword of Mehmet the Conqueror
- Topkapı dagger

TIP

- Don't miss the Fourth Courtyard, with its views over the Bosphorus and Sea of Marmara.

The heartbeat of the Ottoman empire for nearly 400 years, Topkapı Palace is now a museum with extensive collections of imperial porcelain, jewels, costumes and arms.

The palace From 1461, when Mehmet II ordered its construction, to 1856, when the royal family moved to Dolmabahçe (▷ 96–97), Topkapı was both the sultan's private residence and the headquarters of the Ottoman empire. Allow half a day for a visit. You enter through the Imperial Gate, which leads to the First Courtyard, a public area where you will find Aya Irini church (▷ 38). You need to buy a ticket to enter the Second Courtyard, dominated by the Divan (Imperial Council Chamber), where the sultan's advisers met

Clockwise from left: visitors enter the palace; a bell backed by traditional blue tiles; view of the palace, surrounded by greenery; vivid tiling; gilded entrance to the Divan; a mosaic

to discuss matters of state while the sultan watched through a grille in the wall.

The Harem A separate ticket gives access to the Harem, the private quarters of the sultan and his family. This was a palace within a palace, with its own mosques, baths and 300 rooms in a labyrinth of corridors and courtyards, where the imperial wives and concubines were watched over by the *valide sultan* (queen mother). At the heart of the Harem is the Imperial Hall.

The Treasury The Third Courtyard contains the imperial treasures, from dazzling silk costumes to the emerald-studded Topkapı dagger and the sacred relics of the Prophet Muhammad.

THE BASICS

www.topkapisarayi.gov.tr

➕ H9

✉ Topkapı, Sultanahmet

☎ 212-512-0480

🕐 Wed–Mon 9–7. Harem: 10–4

🍴 Café (€), Konyalı restaurant (€€; ▷ 44)

🚌 Sultanahmet

♿ None

💰 Expensive; separate charge for Harem

❓ 30-min guided tour of the Harem must be booked in advance to avoid a long wait

Türk ve Islam Eserleri Müzesi

See a fascinating selection of arts and crafts from the Islamic world

THE BASICS

➕ F11
✉ Ibrahim Paşa Sarayı, At Meydanı 46, Sultanahmet
☎ 212-518-1805
🕐 Tue–Sun 9–4.30
🍴 Café (€)
🚇 Sultanahmet
♿ None
👊 Inexpensive

HIGHLIGHTS

● Audience Hall
● Carved lions and sphinxes
● Brass doorknobs depicting dragons from 12th-century mosque at Cizre
● Iznik tiles
● Engraved Selçuk drum
● Miniature Korans
● 'Holbein' carpet
● Brass lamps
● Yurt dwelling

TIP

● There are views of the Blue Mosque across the Hippodrome from the café terrace in the garden.

Have you ever wondered how the carpet came to be an indispensable item? Do you know how to make sheep's cheese? All is revealed in the Museum of Turkish and Islamic Art's ethnography section.

The palace The museum is housed in the former palace of Süleyman the Magnificent's grand vizier, Ibrahim Paşa, who received it as a gift from the sultan in 1520.

Arts and crafts The museum has an outstanding collection of arts and crafts from the Islamic world. You can see carved window shutters, gilded boxes, lacquered bookbindings and a relief map of the Ottoman empire in 1901.

Carpets Hanging in the former Audience Hall of the palace are carpets from as far afield as Hungary, Persia and Arab Spain, the earliest fragments dating back to the 13th century. Over time the paired birds, animals and tree motifs employed by the Seljuks gave way to more stylized geometrical patterns. This transition is recorded in Western art of the period, so it is appropriate that the designs themselves are named after the artists in whose paintings the carpets appear: Bellini, Van Eyck, Holbein.

Ethnography Carpet-weaving as a domestic handicraft originated with the nomadic peoples of Anatolia. Besides learning about natural dyes, you can visit a yurt, a black goatskin tent and other traditional dwellings.

One of two Medusa heads found here (left); some of the 336 columns (right)

Yerebatan Sarnıcı

The Basilica Cistern can easily be missed because it lies some 6m (19.5ft) below the ground, yet it is one of the most impressive sights in Istanbul. It dates back to AD532.

Imperial reservoir The cistern was built in the reign of the Emperor Justinian, primarily to supply water to the Great Palace. Aqueducts carried the water from its source in the Belgrade Forest, about 19km (12 miles) away. After the Ottoman conquest the cistern fell into disuse, although attempts were made to repair it in the 18th and 19th centuries. It was only in 1987, however, that this magnificent building was finally opened to the public.

Exploring the cistern Water still drips from the ceiling of the imposing, brick-vaulted chamber, although the strategically placed spotlights and specially constructed gangways make exploration easy. The main attraction—apart from the fish that thrive in the remaining several centimetres of water—is the forest of pillars supporting the magnificent arched roof. These columns are by no means uniform. Only about a third of the capitals are Corinthian, for example, while the patterning on one of the pillars resembles teardrops, on another peacock feathers. These inconsistencies suggest that they were removed from other sites and reused here, and might also account for the two Medusa heads found here, one set upside-down, the other lying on its side.

THE BASICS

- G10
- Yerebatan Caddesi, Sultanahmet
- 212-522-1259
- Apr–end Sep daily 9–6.30; Oct–end Mar daily 9–5.30
- Café (€)
- Sultanahmet
- None
- Moderate
- Occasional concerts and plays

HIGHLIGHTS

- Medusa heads
- 336 columns

TIP

- Look for classical concerts taking place in summer—this vast space has magnificent acoustics and the atmosphere of an underground cathedral.

More to See

AHMET III ÇEŞMESI

This rococo fountain, beside the Imperial Gate to Topkapı Palace (▷ 34–35), is the finest in Istanbul. One of many extravagances built at the behest of the Tulip Sultan, Ahmed III, its decoration is exuberant, with bands of tinted marbles, floral reliefs and calligraphic patterning. The inscription reads 'Turn on the tap, drink the water and pray for the house of Ahmed.'

✚ H10 ⊠ Babıhümayun Caddesi, Sultanahmet 🚇 Sultanahmet

AYA IRINI (CHURCH OF DIVINE PEACE)

This sturdy brick church is one of the oldest religious buildings in Istanbul. It was commissioned by Emperor Justinian in AD537, about the same time as Ayasofya (▷ 26–27). Of the once-lavish interior, only a stunning mosaic of Christ on the Cross survives.

✚ H10 ⊠ First Courtyard, Topkapı Sarayı 🍴 Cafés (€) nearby 🚇 Gülhane ♿ Few 🚫 Closed except for concerts (▷ 43)

CAĞALOĞLU HAMAMI

Opened in 1741 in the reign of Mahmut I, these baths are probably the most famous in Istanbul, with a guest list that is claimed to include Franz Liszt, Florence Nightingale and Cameron Diaz. Options range from a self-service bath to 'treatment fit for a sultan', which consists of a luxury body scrub, shampoo and massage.

✚ G10 ⊠ Kazım Ismail Gürkan Caddesi 34, Sultanahmet ☎ 212-522-2424 🕐 Daily 8am–10pm for men; 8–8 for women 🚇 Sultanahmet

DIVAN YOLU

Back in the reign of Constantine the Great this was the main street of Byzantium, known as the Mese (Middle Way). Centuries later it became Divan Yolu (Road of the Divan Council), the traditional Ottoman processional route from the city to Topkapı Palace.

✚ G11 ⊠ Divan Yolu, Sultanahmet 🍴 Cafés (€) and restaurants (€€) 🚇 Sultanahmet, Çemberlitaş

The Ahmet III Fountain dates from 1726

The Church of Divine Peace

GEDIK PAŞA HAMAMI

Dating from 1475, soon after the Ottoman conquest, these baths may well be the oldest in the city. The founder, Gedik Ahmet Paşa, was grand vizier under Mehmet the Conqueror and commander of the Ottoman fleet. The hammam is capped by an impressive dome and flanked by alcoves and cubicles faced with marble.

➕ E11 ✉ Emin Sinan Hamamı Sokağı, Sultanahmet ☎ 212-517-8956 ⏰ Daily 6am–midnight 🚇 Beyazıt

GÜLHANE PARKI

This wooded park in the heart of Sultanahmet was created from the old rose garden of Topkapı Palace (▷ 34–35). Apart from the views of the Bosphorus and the statue of Atatürk, you can admire the Alay Köşkü (Review Pavilion), which is built into the wall by the park's main gate.

➕ H9 ✉ Alemdar Caddesi ⏰ Daily 🍴 Cafés 🚇 Gülhane 🦽 None

HALI VE KILIM MÜZESI

This fabulous collection of ancient carpets and kilims is administered by the General Directorate of Pious Foundations and housed within the precincts of the Blue Mosque (▷ 32–33), in the Imperial Pavilion once used by visiting sultans for prayer.

➕ G11 ✉ Sultanahmet Camii ☎ 212-518-1330 ⏰ Tue–Sat 9–12, 1–4 🍴 Cafés and restaurants (€€) nearby 🚇 Sultanahmet 🦽 Inexpensive 🦽 None

HASEKI HÜRREM HAMAMI

If you want to see the interior of a traditional Turkish hammam without actually having a bath, take a look inside these baths, designed by Mimar Sinan in 1556 for Roxelana, the wife of Süleyman the Magnificent. The baths are now used as a state-run carpet store (▷ 42).

➕ G11 ✉ Ayasofya Meydanı 4 ☎ 212-638-0035 ⏰ Summer daily 9–6.30; winter daily 8.30–5.30 🚇 Sultanahmet 🦽 Free 🦽 None

Taking a break in Gülhane Parki

Sultanahmet Walk

Take in the main sights of Sultanahmet on a historical stroll through Ottoman Istanbul.

DISTANCE: 2.5km (1.5 miles) **ALLOW:** 1 hour

START

AT MEYDANI (▷ 25)
✚ G11 🚌 Sultanahmet

END

AT MEYDANI (▷ 25)
✚ G11 🚌 Sultanahmet

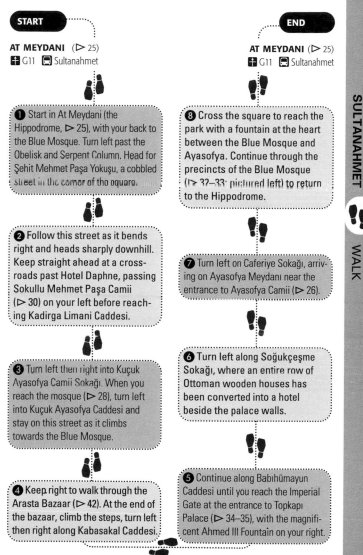

❶ Start in At Meydani (the Hippodrome, ▷ 25), with your back to the Blue Mosque. Turn left past the Obelisk and Serpent Column. Head for Şehit Mehmet Paşa Yokuşu, a cobbled street in the corner of the square.

❷ Follow this street as it bends right and heads sharply downhill. Keep straight ahead at a crossroads past Hotel Daphne, passing Sokullu Mehmet Paşa Camii (▷ 30) on your left before reaching Kadirga Limani Caddesi.

❸ Turn left then right into Küçük Ayasofya Camii Sokağı. When you reach the mosque (▷ 28), turn left into Küçük Ayasofya Caddesi and stay on this street as it climbs towards the Blue Mosque.

❹ Keep right to walk through the Arasta Bazaar (▷ 42). At the end of the bazaar, climb the steps, turn left then right along Kabasakal Caddesi.

❽ Cross the square to reach the park with a fountain at the heart between the Blue Mosque and Ayasofya. Continue through the precincts of the Blue Mosque (▷ 32–33; pictured left) to return to the Hippodrome.

❼ Turn left on Caferiye Sokağı, arriving on Ayasofya Meydanı near the entrance to Ayasofya Camii (▷ 26).

❻ Turn left along Soğukçeşme Sokağı, where an entire row of Ottoman wooden houses has been converted into a hotel beside the palace walls.

❺ Continue along Babıhümayun Caddesi until you reach the Imperial Gate at the entrance to Topkapı Palace (▷ 34–35), with the magnificent Ahmed III Fountain on your right.

Shopping

ARASTA ÇARŞISI

A miniature, more relaxed version of the Grand Bazaar, the Arasta Bazaar has 40 shops selling carpets, jewellery and pottery in the old Ottoman stables beside the Blue Mosque. Unlike the Grand Bazaar, it is open on Sunday.

⊞ G11–12 ⊠ Arasta Çarşısı, Sultanahmet
🔲 Sultanahmet

COCOON

www.cocoontr.com
You cannot miss this shop, with its wacky display of felt hats in all shapes and sizes taking up most of the window.

⊞ G12 ⊠ Küçük Ayasofya Caddesi 13, Sultanahmet
☎ 212-638-6271
🔲 Sultanahmet

DÖSIM

Crafts and souvenir shop run by the Ministry of Culture at the entrance to Topkapı Palace, with a wide range of objects, all at fixed prices.

⊞ H10 ⊠ First Courtyard, Topkapı Sarayı ☎ 212-513-3134 ⊙ Wed–Mon 9–7
🔲 Sultanahmet

ELEGANCE

This smart showroom just off the Hippodrome has wool and silk carpets and kilims from the city of Kayseri, in central Turkey. Prices are not low but staff are knowledgeable and friendly.

⊞ G10 ⊠ Yerebatan Caddesi 46–48, Sultanahmet
☎ 212-511-7527
🔲 Sultanahmet

GALERI CENGIZ

www.galeri-cengiz.com
This shop in the Arasta Çarşısı (▷ this page) has old and new carpets and kilims, as well as accessories made out of kilim material.

⊞ G11 ⊠ Arasta Çarşısı 155–157, Sultanahmet
☎ 212-518-8882
🔲 Sultanahmet

GALERI KAYSERI

With two shops facing each other near the foot of Divan Yolu, Galeri Kayseri offers Sultanahmet's best selection of English-language books about Turkey and Istanbul.

KNOW YOUR CARPETS

First, remember that kilims are woven and have no pile, while carpets are knotted. Second, ask the dealer whether the dyes are natural or synthetic (natural last longer). Third, inspect the tightness of the weave (the greater the number of knots, the more expensive the carpet). Finally, take advice but don't be browbeaten. Choose the pattern and shades that appeal to you most—after all, it is you who has to live with the carpet.

⊞ G11 ⊠ Divan Yolu Caddesi 11 and 58 ☎ 212-512-0456 ⊙ Daily 9–9
🔲 Sultanahmet

HASEKI HAMAMI CARPET AND KILIM SALES STORE

In the historic Haseki Hürrem baths (▷ 39), this carpet salesroom is run by the Ministry of Culture. Prices are clearly marked and haggling is not expected. Come here first to get a feel for prices before heading for the Grand Bazaar.

⊞ G11 ⊠ Ayasofya Meydanı 4 ☎ 212-638-0035
🔲 Sultanahmet

ISTANBUL HANDICRAFTS CENTRE

Watch the artists at work in this courtyard bazaar, in an 18th-century *medrese* (religious school) beside the Yeşil Ev hotel. Among the items produced and sold here are calligraphy, glassware, ceramics, Turkish dolls and miniature paintings.

⊞ G11 ⊠ Kabasakal Caddesi, Sultanahmet
☎ 212-517 6782
🔲 Sultanahmet

IZNIK TILES

www.iznikclassics.com
Beautiful hand-painted ceramic tiles and plates, sold from two shops in the Arasta Çarşısı.

⊞ G11 ⊠ Arasta Çarşısı 67, Sultanahmet ☎ 212-517-1705 🔲 Sultanahmet

Entertainment and Nightlife

AYA IRINI

This beautiful 6th-century church is open for concerts during the annual International Music Festival (June and July).

➕ H10 ✉ First Courtyard, Topkapı Sarayı ☎ 212-334-0700 ⏰ Only for concerts 🚇 Gülhane

CAFÉ MEŞALE

Set in a sunken courtyard in the shadow of the Blue Mosque, this attractive outdoor café has cushions, rugs and low stools where you can listen to live folk music or watch dervish dancing displays most evenings. In common with other tea gardens, it serves Turkish tea, coffee and water pipes but no alcohol.

➕ G11 ✉ Arasta Çarşısı 45, Sultanahmet ☎ 212-518-9562 ⏰ Daily 24 hours 🚇 Sultanahmet

CAĞALOĞLU HAMAMI

See page 38.

DERVIŞ

A delightful tea garden opposite the Blue Mosque, with whirling dervish performances every night in summer.

➕ G11 ✉ Kabasakal Caddesi 1, Sultanahmet ☎ 212-516-1465 ⏰ Daily 9am–11pm 🚇 Sultanahmet

GEDIK PAŞA HAMAMI

See page 39.

HAVUZBAŞI

This sunken tea garden with a fountain and views of the Blue Mosque has live Turkish folk music every night in summer.

➕ F12 ✉ Nakilbent Sokağı 2, Sultanahmet ☎ 212-638-8819 ⏰ Daily 10am–midnight

ORIENT HOSTEL

This backpacker's hostel (▷ 109) in the Cankurtaran district of Sultanahmet has live belly-dancing three times a week, in a basement bar or on the rooftop terrace in summer.

WHAT'S ON

To find out what's on while you're in Istanbul, pick up a copy of the monthly *Time Out Istanbul*, which is published in Turkish- and English-language editions. The easiest way of getting tickets is from the box office of the various venues, but tickets for arts and sports events are also available through Biletix (☎ 216-556-9800; www.biletix.com). Biletix has ticket outlets throughout the city, including Vakkorama in the Akmerkez shopping mall (▷ 104) and at the Istiklal Kitabevi bookshop, found at Istiklal Caddesi 79–81.

➕ H11 ✉ Akbıyık Caddesi 13, Sultanahmet ☎ 212-517-9493 ⏰ Mon, Wed, Fri 11pm 🚇 Sultanahmet

ORIENT HOUSE

www.orienthouseistanbul.com
Not to be confused with Orient Hostel (▷ this page), this place offers extravagant dinner shows in an old Ottoman hall, with belly-dancing, folk and wedding dances, whirling dervishes and a military-style Janissary band, accompanied by a four-course meal with beer or wine included

➕ D11 ✉ Tiyatro Caddesi 27 ☎ 212-517-3488 ⏰ Daily 9pm–midnight 🚇 Beyazıt

SET ÜSTÜ

Tea served in brass pots, with fabulous views over Seraglio Point and the Bosphorus from this tea garden near the Kennedy Caddesi entrance to Gülhane Park.

➕ J8 ✉ Gülhane Parkı ⏰ Daily 9–9 🚇 Gülhane

YENI MARMARA

A traditional café, where local people sip Turkish coffee, play backgammon and smoke waterpipes on a summer terrace overlooking the Sea of Marmara.

➕ G12 ✉ Çayiroğlu Sokağı, Sultanahmet ☎ 212-516-9013 ⏰ Daily 8am–midnight 🚇 Sultanahmet

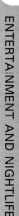

Restaurants

PRICES

Prices are approximate, based on a three-course meal for one person.

€€€	over 40 YTL
€€	20–40 YTL
€	under 20 YTL

AMEDROS (€€)

You'll find pasta, steaks and an international menu at this busy Sultanahmet restaurant. The house special is *testi* kebab, lamb cooked in a clay pot that is smashed open at your table.

🗺 F10 ✉ Hoca Rüstem Sokağı, Divan Yolu Caddesi ☎ 212-522-8356 🕐 Daily 12 11 🚇 Sultanahmet

BEYAZ (€€€)

Unlike most restaurants in Kumkapı, this is right on the port, with views across the Sea of Marmara, and fresh fish from the nearby market.

🗺 D12 ✉ Balıkcılar Çarşısı 28, Kennedy Caddesi, Kumkapı ☎ 212-518-3631 🕐 Daily 12–12 🚇 Kumkapı

DOY-DOY (€)

Filling menu of kebabs, salad and *lahmacun* (Turkish pizza) in the backstreets, downhill from the Hippodrome. There's a view of the Blue Mosque from the rooftop terrace, plus a lounge with sofas, cushions and mint tea.

🗺 G12 ✉ Şifa Hamamı Sokağı 13, Sultanahmet ☎ 212-517-1588 🕐 Daily 9am–11pm 🚇 Sultanahmet

KONYALI (€€)

The attraction here is the setting, in the grounds of Topkapı Palace with views over the Bosphorus. Get here early for the Turkish cuisine, before the tour parties arrive.

🗺 J9 ✉ Fourth Courtyard, Topkapı Sarayı ☎ 212-513-9696 🕐 Wed–Mon 10–5 🚇 Sultanahmet

RAMI (€€€)

Contemporary Ottoman cuisine in a restored wooden house, with

KUMKAPI

The ancient port of Kumkapı has the highest concentration of fish restaurants in Istanbul. There are well over 50, mostly crowded around the main square. There are spectacular views of the Marmara from the fish market on Kennedy Caddesi, but if it's atmosphere you're after, head inland behind the railway station, where tables spill out onto the street and gypsy musicians serenade you while you dine. With its twinkling lights, flower sellers, fountains and cobbled streets, Kumkapı buzzes on summer evenings.

fabulous views of the Blue Mosque from the rooftop terrace.

🗺 G11 ✉ Utangaç Sokağı 6 ☎ 212-517-6593 🕐 Daily 12–12 🚇 Sultanahmet

RUMELI CAFÉ (€€)

Traditional Turkish cooking with a Mediterranean twist. There's a warm fire in the winter and tables on the street in summer.

🗺 G10 ✉ Ticatherane Sokağı, Divan Yolu Caddesi ☎ 212-512-0008 🕐 Daily 12–12 🚇 Sultanahmet

SARNIÇ (€€€)

High-class Turkish cuisine in a converted Roman cistern behind Ayasofya, now brilliantly restored and highly atmospheric when lit by candles at night.

🗺 H10 ✉ Soğukçeşme Sokağı 6 ☎ 212-512-4291 🕐 Daily 7pm–10.30pm 🚇 Gülhane

TARIHI SULTANAHMET KÖFTECISI (€)

Opened in 1920 and still serving the same no-nonsense menu of *köfte* (meatballs), kebabs, salads, beans and rice to crowds of satisfied customers.

🗺 G11 ✉ Divan Yolu Caddesi 12, Sultanahmet ☎ 212-520-0566 🕐 Daily 12–10 🚇 Sultanahmet

With hawkers selling inexpensive goods by the quayside and ferries chugging across the mouth of the Golden Horn, Eminönü marks the start of the sprawling Bazaar Quarter, whose steep streets climb the slopes to the labyrinthine Grand Bazaar.

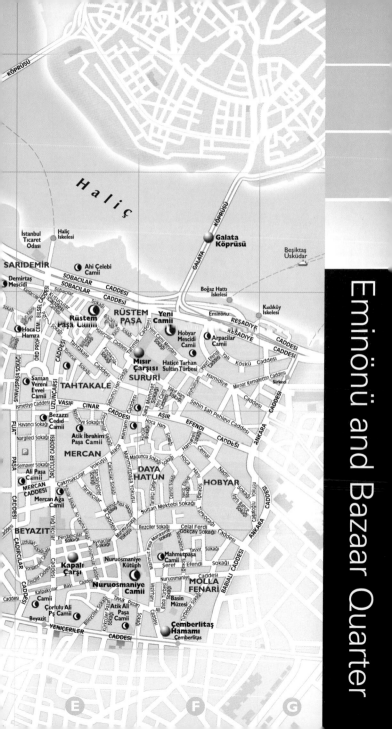

Haliç

KÖPRÜSÜ

İstanbul
Ticaret
Odası

Haliç
İskelesi

Galata
Köprüsü

Beşiktaş
Üsküdar

SARIDEMIR

Ahi Çelebi
Camii

Demirtaş
Mescidi

SOBACILAR

SOBACILAR CADDESİ

Boğaz Hattı
İskelesi

Kadıköy
İskelesi

Eminönü

REŞADİYE

CADDESİ

Hoca
Hamza

RÜSTEM
PAŞA

Rüstem
Paşa Camii

Yeni
Camii

Hobyar
Mescidi
Camii

Arpacılar
Camii

Köskü   Caddesi

Mısır
Çarşısı

Hatice Turhan
Sultan Türbesi

Hamidiye

Mimar Kemalettin Caddesi

Sirkeci

CADDESİ

ANKARA

Saman
Vereni
Evvel
Camii

TAHTAKALE

SURURİ

VASIF   ÇINAR

CADDESİ

AŞIR

EFENDİ

CADDESİ

Bezazzı
Cedid
Camii

Atik İbrahim
Paşa Camii

MERCAN

DAYA
HATUN

HOBYAR

Ali Paşa

MERCAN
CADDESİ

Mercan Ağa
Camii

BEYAZIT

ÇADIRCILAR

Kapalı
Çarşı

Nuruosmaniye
Kütüph

Mahmutpaşa
Camii

MOLLA
FENARİ

Nuruosmaniye
Camii

BABIALI CADDESİ

Camii

Çorlulu Ali
Pş Camii

Atik Ali
Paşa
Camii

Basın
Müzesi

Beyazıt

Çemberlitaş
Hamamı

YENİÇERİLER

CADDESİ

Çemberlitaş

E   F   G

Eminönü and Bazaar Quarter

Beyazıt Meydanı

Left to right: a street vendor; Beyazıt's mausoleum; shoppers carrying a newly purchased carpet

THE BASICS

🔲 D10
✉ Beyazıt Meydanı
🍴 Lively café scene in nearby streets
🚇 Beyazıt

HIGHLIGHTS

● University Gate (Calligraphy Museum, ▷ 57)
● Forum Taurii ruins
● Mosque courtyard

TIP

● A lane behind the mosque contains the Sahaflar Çarşısı (Booksellers' Bazaar), where books have been traded since Ottoman times. Students from the nearby university come here to buy textbooks; stalls also sell framed calligraphy and antique coins.

This large open square on the site of the Roman forum is a great place to take the pulse of the city.

The square Beyazıt Meydanı, one of Istanbul's busiest squares, occupies the site of the Forum Taurii, once a thriving Byzantine marketplace–you can see some remains of it on the other side of Ordu Caddesi, part of the Roman street known as the Mese. Today the square contains the ceremonial gateway to Istanbul University and the Beyazıt Mosque *medrese*, now the Calligraphy Museum (▷ 57).

The mosque The graceful Beyazıt Mosque was built between 1501 and 1506 in the reign of Beyazıt II, making it the oldest surviving Ottoman mosque in Istanbul. You will find Beyazıt's *türbe* (mausoleum) in the cemetery behind the mosque. The architect of this magnificent complex, Yakub Şah, clearly had an eye for detail as well as an instinct for geometrical proportion. He used these gifts to brilliant effect in the colonnaded courtyard, where the columns of contrasting red, grey and green marble are crowned with stalactite decoration. Yakub Şah based the interior on the Christian church of Ayasofya. Four massive piers support the central dome, which is flanked by two semi-domes. The *mimbar* (staircase), mihrab and beautifully sculptured balustrade are original 16th-century features, as is the sultan's loge, to the right of the *mimbar*, which rests on columns of precious marble.

Treat yourself to a Turkish bath or massage

Çemberlitaş Hamamı

This magnificent bathhouse is the best place to initiate yourself into the delights of the Turkish bath.

The baths The baths were founded in 1584 by Valide Sultan Nurbanu, the widow of Sultan Selim II, and have been in continuous use ever since. Designed by architect Mimar Sinan, they remain one of the finest examples of 16th-century Ottoman civil architecture in Istanbul. The baths are divided into the traditional male and female sections, with marble alcoves and washbasins around a central *hararet* (steam room), where sunlight filters in through star-shaped skylights in the dome.

Beginner's guide On arrival, you will be shown into the *camekan*, a courtyard with wooden cubicles around the edge, where you should undress and leave your clothes. The attendant will give you a *peştemal*, a cotton towel to wrap around your body, and a pair of slippers. You pass through the *soğukluk* (cool room) on your way to the *hararet*, where you lie and sweat for about 15 minutes on a heated marble platform known as a *göbek taşı* (navel stone). If you have chosen the massage, an attendant will then pummel and knead your body, scrub your skin with a coarse *kese* (mitten) and wash you all over with soap. Afterwards, you are free to relax in the *hararet* (steam room) for as long as you like before returning to the *camekan* to collect your clothes.

THE BASICS

www.cemberlitashamami.com.tr

🔳 F10

✉ Vezirhanı Caddesi 8

☎ 212-522-7974

🕐 Daily 6am–midnight

🚇 Çemberlitaş

💳 Expensive

TIPS

● You can choose between a self-service bath and a massage. Both are enjoyable, but for the full hammam experience, it is worth paying extra for the massage at least once.

● Take plenty of change as the masseurs and cloakroom attendants will all expect a tip.

Grand Bazaar

Kapalı Çarşı

HIGHLIGHTS

- İç Bedesten
- Zincirli Han
- Mosques, baths and fountains

TIPS

- Visit on Wednesday at 1pm, when a carpet auction takes place in the Sandal Bedesten.
- Prices are not fixed and the traders are skilled at bargaining, so you need patience and good humour to negotiate a purchase.

The Covered Bazaar, usually referred to as the Grand Bazaar, was built after the Ottoman conquest as the city's main market—making it perhaps the world's oldest shopping mall.

İç Bedesten The bazaar is a labyrinth of seemingly endless vaulted arcades and passageways lined with merchants selling their wares—a city within a city. At the heart of the market is the İç Bedesten, which dates from the period of the Ottoman conquest (1456–61). An enormous warehouse surrounded by market stalls and workshops, it was once covered by canvas awnings. Today it deals in Ottoman antiques.

Orientation Traditionally, certain streets specialize in the sale of particular items—Halıcılar

There's plenty to buy at the Grand Bazaar, from carpets and brassware to traditional tiles and eye-catching slippers

Caddesi, for example, means 'Carpet-Sellers' Street'. If you are looking for leatherware, head for Keseciler Caddesi; if it's gold and silverware you are after, try Kalpakçılar Caddesi. The range of goods on sale is astonishing: hand-painted bowls, brass lamps, embroidered waistcoats, T-shirts, kilim bags, meerschaum pipes and the ubiquitous amulets to ward off the 'evil eye'. Shopping in the bazaar can be tiring, but there are many cafés where you can join the traders taking tea or enjoying a game of backgammon.

Hans Don't leave the bazaar without taking a detour into the picturesque courtyards of the old *hans* or caravanserais, built originally to accommodate merchants. The ground floors of these arcaded buildings, once stables and storerooms, are now used as workshops.

THE BASICS

www.kapalicarsi.org.tr
➕ E10
✉ Kapalı Çarşı, Beyazıt
☎ 212-522-3173
🕐 Mon–Sat 8.30–7
🍴 Restaurants (€€) and cafés (€)
🚋 Tram to Çemberlitaş or Beyazıt
♿ None
🆓 Free

Mısır Çarşısı

Spice Bazaar

TOP 25

Enjoy the aroma of herbs and spices as you shop in the Spice Bazaar

KEKİK OREGANO

THE BASICS

🗺 F8

✉ Yeni Camii Meydanı, Eminönü

🕐 Mon–Sat 9–7

🍴 Pandeli restaurant (€€; lunch only; ▷ 62)

🚊 Eminönü

🚌 Eminönü

♿ None

🖐 Free

HIGHLIGHTS

● Pistachio-filled Turkish delight
● Honeycomb
● Saffron
● Caviar from Azerbaijan
● Nuts and dried fruit
● Brass pepper mills

TIP

● Take time to explore the streets around the bazaar, with their delicatessens, coffee shops and fresh produce markets.

The Spice Bazaar makes for a more relaxing shopping trip than the Grand Bazaar because it's easier to find your way around. See how much Turkish delight you can sample before having to buy some.

Egyptian Bazaar Completed in 1663 for Turhan Hatice Sultan, mother of Mehmet IV, the Spice Bazaar was intended to provide income for the charitable foundations of the nearby Yeni Mosque (▷ 57). The source of this income was the import duties levied on the spices as they passed through Egypt (which was at that time part of the Ottoman empire), which is why the Turks still call this the Egyptian Bazaar.

Turkish delight The entrance to the bazaar is through one of four robust, double-arched gates. Of the shops here today, only a few specialize exclusively in herbs and spices; even so, the aroma is unmistakable, a heady mix of saffron, coriander, ginger, cinnamon, paprika, sage and tamarind. The second overwhelming impression is the riot of colour. You will see hanging aubergines (eggplants), paprika and salamis, trays filled with sweets, nuts, dried figs and apricots, and counters stacked with red, yellow, blue and green pots of caviar. Few can resist the Turkish delight, with its hazelnut and pistachio fillings; or the tea, scented with apples, oranges, lemons, cherries, cinnamon and rose-hip.

Richly decorated Iznik tiles line the walls of the Rüstem Paşa Mosque

This is the best place in Istanbul to learn to love the tile-maker's art. If you can, visit the gallery, where you will find examples of the architect Mimar Sinan's original designs, which were considered too restrained by Rüstem Paşa.

The mosque This little gem of a mosque dates from 1561. It was designed by Sinan for Süleyman the Magnificent's son-in-law, Grand Vizier Rüstem Paşa, although he never lived to see it completed. The charitable institutions of the *külliye* were financed by the vaulted shops that Sinan constructed at street level below the expansive terrace leading to the mosque itself. Space was at a premium in the city's commercial quarter, so the courtyard area is restricted to a highly unusual double porch. The sloping roof is supported by a row of delicately carved stone pillars.

Decoration Sinan planned the prayer hall as an octagon inscribed within a rectangle. The main dome is flanked by four semi-domes, one at each corner of the building, and rests on four massive octagonal columns and four pillars abutting on the east and west walls. There are galleries on the north and south sides. Following Rüstem Paşa's death, his widow, Mihrimah Sultan, spared no expense on the decoration of the mosque. Every available space is set with exquisite Iznik tiles, designed by artists at the palace's own workshops and featuring extravagant geometric and floral motifs.

THE BASICS

➕ E8
✉ Hasırcılar Caddesi, Eminönü
🕐 Hours of prayer
🍴 Cafés (€) nearby
🚊 Eminönü
🚢 Eminönü
♿ None
💰 Free/donation

HIGHLIGHTS

● Terrace
● Double porch
● Carved stone capitals (porch)
● Lozenge capitals (prayer hall)
● Dome
● Iznik tiles
● Octagonal columns
● Calligraphic shields under dome

Süleymaniye Camii

HIGHLIGHTS

● Four minarets with 10 balconies, symbolizing Süleyman's position as the fourth sultan after the Conquest, and the tenth Ottoman sultan overall
● *Medreses*
● Dome of mosque
● Iznik tiles on mihrab wall
● Mausoleum of Süleyman the Magnificent
● Mausoleum of Haseki Hürrem Sultan

Mimar Sinan's masterpiece was built for his patron, Süleyman the Magnificent, who is buried in a mausoleum in the garden alongside his wife Haseki Hürrem, better known as Roxelana.

Külliye With the construction of the Süleymaniye Mosque complex between 1550 and 1559, the architect Sinan finally emancipated himself from the influence of Ayasofya to reveal his astonishing originality. In the 16th century the entire compound would have hummed with activity—within its precincts were four *medreses*, schools, kitchens, shops, baths and a caravanserai. Life is returning to the Süleymaniye as some of the buildings are restored; the Evvel and Sani *medreses*, for example, have been converted into one of

Clockwise from left: the dome of the Süleymaniye Camii; people walking through the porticoed courtyard to the entrance; the octagonal mausoleum of Süleyman, built after his death in 1566; buttresses supporting the central dome; the şadirvan (fountain for ritual ablutions); Muslims cleansing their feet before entering

Istanbul's most important libraries, while the *imaret* (soup kitchen) is now a restaurant.

Interior The prayer hall is a perfect square, and the diameter of the dome is exactly half its height. The other elements in the composition—semi-domes and cupolas, window-lit tympana, galleries and pillars—dance in attendance around this feature. There is little sculptural decoration, but Sinan has allowed other artists free rein, especially on the mihrab wall with its marbles, calligraphy and magnificent stained-glass windows. We know the identity of some artists. The calligrapher (who apparently went blind in the process) was Ahmet Karahisarı; the windows were designed by Ibrahim Sarhoş ('the Drunkard'); the woodwork, inlaid with ivory and mother-of-pearl, is by Ustad Ahmed.

THE BASICS

⊞ D8
⊠ Süleymaniye Caddesi, Süleymaniye
⏰ Hours of prayer
🚇 Beyazıt
♿ None
💷 Free/donation

TIP

● Have lunch at Darüzziyafe (▷ 62), the former soup kitchen, now a restaurant with an attractive courtyard garden.

More to See

BOZDOĞAN KEMERI (AQUEDUCT OF VALENS)

This impressive double-arched aqueduct was built in the fourth century AD by Emperor Valens to carry water across the valley between the fourth and the third hills (Fatih to Beyazıt). About 625m (681 yards) of the 1km (0.5 miles) remain and can be seen to best advantage from the grounds of the Şehzade Camii.

➕ B8 ✉ Atatürk Bulvari

GALATA KÖPRÜSÜ

Spanning the mouth of the Golden Horn, Galata Bridge is a city landmark. Fishermen dangle their rods from the bridge, ferries bustle to and fro, and restaurants on the lower terraces offer waterfront dining and romantic sunset views. The bridge was built in 1992 after an earlier, much-loved iron bridge was destroyed by fire. The original bridge was rebuilt upstream between Balat and Hasköy and is now called Eski Galata Köprüsü (Old Galata Bridge).

➕ F7 🚢 Eminönü, Karaköy

KALENDERHANE CAMII

The 12th-century Byzantine Church of Theotokos Kiriotissa (Our Lady Mother of God) has been painstakingly restored by archaeologists. Visiting is restricted but try to get inside to see the surviving marble decoration and mosaic fragments, including the Theotokos Kiriotissa herself and reputedly the earliest fresco depiction of St. Francis of Assisi.

➕ C9 ✉ 16 Mart Şehitleri Caddesi, Eminönü 🕐 Open during hours of prayer 🚫 None 💲 Free

MIMAR SINAN TÜRBESI

There can be no more fitting memorial to the 16th-century architect of Süleymaniye Camii, Mimar Sinan (▷ 54), than this modest mausoleum, designed by Sinan himself and standing outside the mosque in what used to be the garden of his home.

➕ D8 ✉ Mimar Sinan Caddesi, Süleymaniye 🕐 Mon–Sat 8.30–5 💲 Free

Cars and passers-by are dwarfed by the arches of the Aqueduct of Valens

Dusk on Galata Bridge

NURUOSMANIYE CAMII

Casting a shadow across the Nuruosmaniye Gate of the Covered Bazaar is the mosque that gives it its name, possibly the finest piece of Ottoman baroque architecture in Istanbul. It was completed in 1755 in the reign of Osman III.

➕ E10 ✉ Nuruosmaniye Caddesi, Çemberlitaş ⏱ Hours of prayer 🚍 Çemberlitaş ♿ None 💷 Free

ŞEHZADE CAMII

The 'Prince's Mosque' was built in the 1540s to commemorate Mehmet, son of Süleyman the Magnificent, who died of smallpox aged 21. It was the architect Mimar Sinan's first major commission and has an austere simplicity missing from his later works. The tiling in Mehmet's mausoleum at the side of the mosque is particularly beautiful, creating a paradise garden in green, blue and yellow.

➕ C9 ✉ Şehzadebaşı Caddesi, Şehzadebaşı ⏱ Hours of prayer ♿ None 💷 Free

VAKIF HAT SANATLARI MÜZESI (CALLIGRAPHY MUSEUM)

This is the only museum in the world devoted to the art form of calligraphy. The displays include a reconstruction of a calligraphy workshop.

➕ D10 ✉ Beyazıt Meydanı, Beyazıt ☎ 212-527-5851 ⏱ Tue–Sat 9–4 🍴 Cafés (€) nearby 🚍 Beyazıt ♿ None 💷 Inexpensive

YENI CAMII

This imposing mosque dominates the approaches to Galata Bridge (▷ 56). It was commissioned towards the end of the 16th century, although it was not completed until 1663. The two-floor building on the forecourt is the sultan's 'private pew', actually a suite of luxuriously appointed rooms complete with sea views and a private toilet.

➕ F8 ✉ Yeni Camii Meydanı, Eminönü ⏱ Hours of prayer 🍴 Cafés (€) nearby 🚍 Eminönü ♿ None 💷 Free

The domes of the Şehzade Mosque

A market outside the Yeni Mosque

Two Bazaars

Explore the busy shopping streets of the Tahtakale district on a walk from the Spice Bazaar to the Grand Bazaar.

DISTANCE: 1.5km (1 mile) **ALLOW:** 1 hour

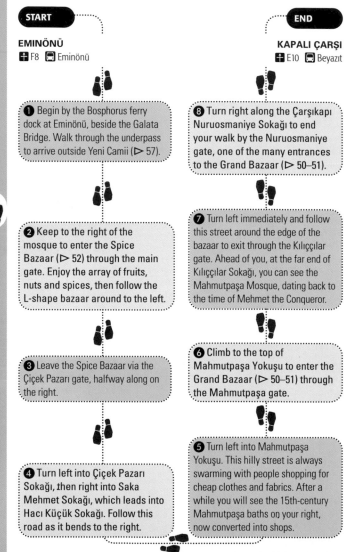

START

EMINÖNÜ
F8 Eminönü

1 Begin by the Bosphorus ferry dock at Eminönü, beside the Galata Bridge. Walk through the underpass to arrive outside Yeni Camii (▷ 57).

2 Keep to the right of the mosque to enter the Spice Bazaar (▷ 52) through the main gate. Enjoy the array of fruits, nuts and spices, then follow the L-shape bazaar around to the left.

3 Leave the Spice Bazaar via the Çiçek Pazarı gate, halfway along on the right.

4 Turn left into Çiçek Pazarı Sokağı, then right into Saka Mehmet Sokağı, which leads into Hacı Küçük Sokağı. Follow this road as it bends to the right.

END

KAPALI ÇARŞI
E10 Beyazıt

8 Turn right along the Çarşıkapı Nuruosmaniye Sokağı to end your walk by the Nuruosmaniye gate, one of the many entrances to the Grand Bazaar (▷ 50–51).

7 Turn left immediately and follow this street around the edge of the bazaar to exit through the Kılıççılar gate. Ahead of you, at the far end of Kılıççılar Sokağı, you can see the Mahmutpaşa Mosque, dating back to the time of Mehmet the Conqueror.

6 Climb to the top of Mahmutpaşa Yokuşu to enter the Grand Bazaar (▷ 50–51) through the Mahmutpaşa gate.

5 Turn left into Mahmutpaşa Yokuşu. This hilly street is always swarming with people shopping for cheap clothes and fabrics. After a while you will see the 15th-century Mahmutpaşa baths on your right, now converted into shops.

Shopping

ABDULLA

You'll find everything you need for a relaxing Turkish bath—silk and cotton *peştemals* (bath wraps) and towels, olive oil soap—in this small shop right at the heart of the Grand Bazaar.

➕ E10 ✉ Halıcılar Caddesi 62, Kapalı Çarşı ☎ 212-527-3684 🚇 Beyazıt

ADNAN & HASAN

Established in 1978, this shop sells carpets and kilims, as well as tribal and nomadic pieces such as grain sacks and camel saddle-bags.

➕ E10 ✉ Halıcılar Caddesi 89, Kapalı Çarşı ☎ 212-527-9887 🚇 Beyazıt

ALI MUHIDDIN HACI BEKIR

The original Turkish delight shop is still going strong after more than 200 years, with a wide variety of gift boxes in tastes ranging from rosewater to lemon, hazelnut and pistachio.

➕ F8 ✉ Hamidiye Caddesi 83, Eminönü ☎ 212-522-0666 🕐 Mon–Sat 8–8, Sun 9–8 🚇 Eminönü

DELI KIZIN YERI

www.delikiz.com
The first shop in the Grand Bazaar to be owned by an American woman sells scarves, dolls and children's gifts, handmade in the shop's own workshop and inspired by Turkish designs. The name of the shop means 'crazy lady'.

➕ E10 ✉ Halıcılar Caddesi 82, Kapalı Çarşı ☎ 212-526-1251 🚇 Beyazıt

DERVIŞ

www.dervis.com
Similar to Abdulla (▷ this page), Derviş sells eco-friendly bath accessories, organic cotton dressing gowns and natural cosmetics from two shops in the Grand Bazaar. Prices are fixed so there is no need to haggle.

➕ E10 ✉ Keseciler Caddesi 33 and Halıcılar Caddesi 51, Kapalı Çarşı ☎ 212-514-4525 🚇 Beyazıt

ETHNICON

www.ethnicon.com
Symbolizing the changing face of the Grand Bazaar, Ethnicon sells contemporary kilims

---

TURKISH DELIGHT

A box of Turkish delight from Istanbul is always a popular gift. Invented by Ali Muhiddin in 1777 and still sold from the original shop, this sticky treat quickly became popular at the Ottoman court. Known in Turkish as *lokum* (morsel), it is sold all over the city in many shades and tastes, though the most common is probably the pink variety scented with rosewater.

---

and rugs for the modern home, at fixed prices.

➕ E10 ✉ Takkeciler Sokağı 58–60, Kapalı Çarşı ☎ 212-527-6841 🚇 Beyazıt

HAFIZ MUSTAFA

Directly opposite its better-known rival (Ali Muhiddin Haci Bekir, ▷ this page), this shop also specializes in Turkish delight, which comes in attractively wrapped packages at affordable prices.

➕ F8 ✉ Hamidiye Caddesi 84, Eminönü ☎ 212-513-3610 🕐 Mon–Sat 8–8, Sun 9–8 🚇 Eminönü

KAPALI ÇARŞI (GRAND BAZAAR)

See pages 50–51.

KOÇ DERI

There are dozens of outlets in the Grand Bazaar specializing in leather goods, but this is one of the best, with a wide selection of leather jackets and bags. There are several other leather shops on the same street.

➕ E10 ✉ Kürkçüler Çarşısı, Kapalı Çarşı ☎ 212-527-5553 🚇 Beyazıt

KURAKAHVECI MEHMET EFENDI

Just outside the Tahmis entrance to the Spice Bazaar, this is the place to come for Turkish coffee, which arrives with helpful instructions on how to make it. You can also pick up coffee

cups and a *cezve*, a long-handled brass pot for making coffee.

🔒 E8 ✉ Tahmis Sokağı 66, Eminönü ☎ 212-511-4262 🚇 Eminönü

MALATYA PAZARI

The biggest shop in the Spice Bazaar specializes in sun-dried apricots from Malatya, in eastern Turkey, as well as pistachios, cranberries, stuffed figs and other delicious treats.

🔒 F8 ✉ Mısır Çarşısı 40–44 ☎ 212-520-0440 🚇 Eminönü

MISIR ÇARŞISI

See page 52.

ÖMER GÜNÇE

This is one of the many shops in the Grand Bazaar specializing in inlaid wood backgammon and chess sets. The best are carved out of walnut wood and inlaid with mother-of-pearl.

🔒 E10 ✉ Kavaflar Sokağı 30–32, Kapalı Çarşı ☎ 212-527-5631 🚇 Beyazıt

PUNTO

One attraction here is the setting, in a 17th-century caravanserai, or trading inn, close to the Grand Bazaar; the other is the selection of old and new carpets from all over Turkey.

🔒 F10 ✉ Gazi Sinanpaşa Sokağı 17 ☎ 212-511-0853 🚇 Çemberlitaş

SAHAFLAR ÇARŞISI

This pretty little lane behind the Beyazıt Mosque has been home to booksellers since Ottoman times, and now houses a market of second-hand and antiquarian books, as well as calligraphy and framed Koranic verses.

🔒 D10 ✉ Sahaflar Çarşısı Sokağı, Beyazıt 🕐 Daily 8–8 🚇 Beyazıt

ŞENGÖR

This is one of the oldest, best-respected carpet dealers in Istanbul, founded in 1918, and now in the fifth generation of the same family. From two shops in the Grand Bazaar it sells carpets and kilims from Turkey and Central Asia.

🔒 E10 ✉ Takkeciler Sokağı 65, Kapalı Çarşı ☎ 212 527 2192 🚇 Çemberlitaş

ŞİŞKO OSMAN

www.siskoosman.com
This fourth-generation family business has the largest selection of handmade carpets and

OPENING HOURS

Like most shops in Istanbul, the Grand Bazaar and Spice Bazaar are closed on Sunday. The usual shopping hours are Monday to Saturday 9am–7pm, though many shops in Sultanahmet stay open late in the evening and on Sunday in summer.

kilims from all over Turkey, and can also design and ship rugs to order for overseas customers. Many of their carpets are original dowry pieces created by Anatolian village women as part of their trousseau, and almost all use natural dyes. The main shop takes up most of Zincirli Han, a historic caravanserai around a pretty courtyard in the Grand Bazaar.

🔒 E10 ✉ Zincirli Han 15, Kapalı Çarşı ☎ 212-528-3548 🚇 Beyazıt

SOFA

www.kashifsofa.com
This Aladdin's Cave near the Grand Bazaar is packed with old maps and prints, Kütahya pottery, calligraphy, silverware and other antiques.

🔒 F10 ✉ Nuruosmaniye Caddesi 85 ☎ 212-520-2850 🚇 Çemberlitaş

YURDAN

This company sells new and antique rugs from Turkey and Iran, as well as ethnic jewellery and clothes, from a shop at the heart of the Grand Bazaar—in the Sandal Bedesten, where the weekly carpet auctions take place.

🔒 E10 ✉ Sandal Bedesten 32–34, Kapalı Çarşı ☎ 212-514-1062 🚇 Beyazıt

Entertainment and Nightlife

ÇEMBERLITAŞ HAMAMI
See page 49.

ERENLER
Follow a sign to the 'Mystic Waterpipe Garden' to enter a pretty *medrese* court-yard, with carpet shops down one side and a tea garden on the other. It's popular with both tourists and students from Istanbul.
➕ E10 ✉ Yeniçeriler Caddesi 36, Beyazıt ☎ 212-528-3785 🕐 Daily 7am–midnight 🚇 Beyazıt

LALE BAHÇESI
Walk down the steps to this sunken garden beside the Süleymaniye Mosque, with a tinkling fountain at the middle —just the place to relax on a cushioned bench with a glass of sweet Turkish tea.
➕ D8 ✉ Şifahane Sokağı, Süleymaniye ☎ 212-528-3785 🕐 Daily 8am–midnight

SÜLEYMANIYE HAMAMI
These baths were designed by Mimar Sinan as part of the Süleymaniye Mosque complex. Unusually, they are mixed-sex, which means men and women bathe together, though all the masseurs are male. This makes the baths a good choice for couples, but single women may feel uncomfortable here. A free transfer from your hotel is included in the price.
➕ D8 ✉ Mimar Sinan Caddesi, Süleymaniye ☎ 212-519-5569 🕐 Daily 7am–midnight

Restaurants

PRICES
Prices are approximate, based on a three-course meal for one person.
€€€   over 40 YTL
€€   20–40 YTL
€   under 20 YTL

DARÜZZIYAFE (€€)
Traditional Turkish cuisine in the Süleymaniye Mosque *imaret* (soup kitchen), and courtyard garden. No alcohol.
➕ D8 ✉ Şifahane Sokağı 6, Süleymaniye ☎ 212-511-8415 🕐 Daily 12–11

HAMDI ET LOKANTASI (€€)
A cake shop masks the entrance to this

BALIK EKMEK
The quintessential Istanbul street food is *balık ekmek* (fish in bread), a grilled mackerel sandwich traditionally sold straight from the fishing boats beside Galata Bridge. These days the sandwich is mainly sold from stalls on the quayside, but the aroma of grilled fish still hangs over Eminönü each evening. A portion of *balık ekmek* with salad makes an inexpensive, filling and delicious snack. Sprinkle with salt and lemon juice, then sit down on a bench to enjoy the view.

excellent restaurant, serving kebabs, grilled meat and Turkish dishes, on a rooftop terrace with views of Galata Bridge and the Golden Horn.
➕ E8 ✉ Kalçin Sokağı 17, Eminönü ☎ 212-528-0390 🕐 Daily 12–11pm

PANDELI (€€)
Housed in the former guardhouse of the Spice Bazaar and decorated with blue ceramic tiles, this famous restaurant specializes in aubergine (eggplant) *börek* and sea bass *en papillotte*.
➕ F8 ✉ Mısır Çarşısı 1, Eminönü ☎ 212-527-3909 🕐 Mon–Sat 12–4 🚇 Eminönü

The traditional religious districts of Fener, Balat and Eyüp lie on the south bank of the Haliç (Golden Horn). They form a fascinating area of churches, mosques and historic Greek and Jewish districts within the city walls.

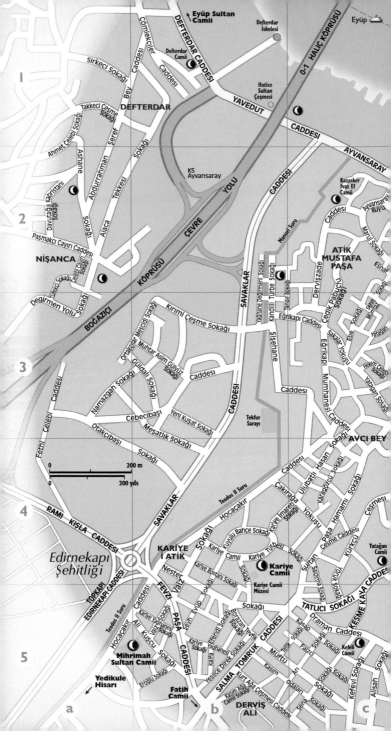

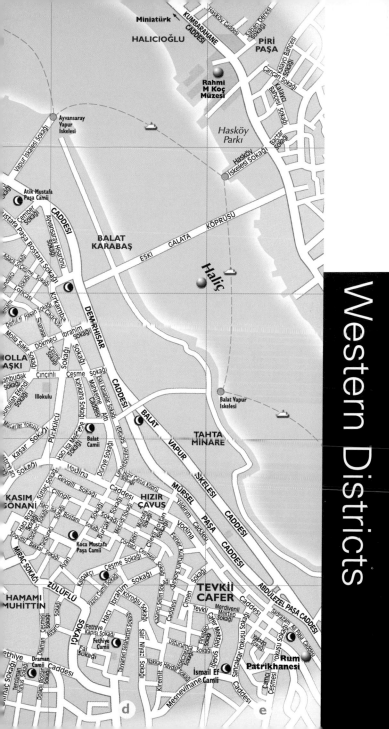

Western Districts

Eyüp Sultan Camii

HIGHLIGHTS

● Wishing window
● Prophet's footprint

TIP

● Take the cable car behind the mosque to the Pierre Loti Café, named after a 19th-century French writer and naval officer who lived in Istanbul and loved the views over the Golden Horn from this spot.

Eyüp is one of the holiest sites in Islam. Crowds of pilgrims descend here on Fridays and religious holidays to make their devotions. The market stalls along the route to the mosque do a brisk trade in religious paraphernalia.

Shrine Eyüp Ensari, standard-bearer and close companion of the Prophet Muhammad, fell in battle during the Arab siege of Constantinople in AD674–78. His burial place was rediscovered in 1453 by Akşemseddin, tutor of Mehmet the Conqueror, and the delighted sultan erected a shrine on the site.

Mosque and *türbe* (mausoleum) The original mosque was destroyed during the earthquake of 1766 and rebuilt by Selim III. A fine example

This striking mosque complex includes the mausoleum of Eyüp Ensari, close friend of the Prophet Muhammad, and is one of the most sacred sites in Islam

of Ottoman baroque, the interior is highlighted with gold leaf on white marble. Many young boys come here on Sunday morning, dressed in white suits for their circumcision. After praying at the mosque, pious Muslims make their way to the octagonal mausoleum of Eyüp Ensari. Dating from 1485, the *türbe* is decorated with blue, white and henna-red tiles from Iznik and Kütahya. Worshippers pause at the 'wishing window' (protected by a golden grille) before filing past the sarcophagus. Preserved in one corner is a cast of the Prophet Muhammad's footprint.

Cemetery A stroll through the hillside cemetery, its faded marble tombstones and crooked stelae half-hidden by cypresses, is a perfect way to round off a visit.

THE BASICS

⊞ Off map at b1

✉ Camii Kebir Caddesi, Eyüp

🕐 Mosque: hours of prayer. Mausoleum of Eyüp: daily 9.30–4.30

🍴 Lots of cafés and restaurants (€) nearby; Pierre Loti Café (▷ Tip, 66)

🚢 Eyüp Vapur Iskelesi

🚫 None

💰 Free/donation

❓ No photography in Eyüp mausoleum

67

Kariye Camii

HIGHLIGHTS

- Christ Pantocrator (mosaic)
- Miracle at Cana (mosaic)
- Metochites presenting Chora to Christ (mosaic)
- Last Judgement (fresco)
- Resurrection (fresco)
- Mother of God (fresco)

TIP

- Asitane (▷ 74) in the Kariye Hotel makes a delightful spot for lunch after visiting the church.

The lovely old Church of St. Saviour of Chora houses some of the world's most precious Byzantine mosaics and frescos. The dramatic rendering of the Resurrection in the apse seems to speak directly to us across seven centuries.

Metochites' church The Church of St. Saviour in Chora (now the Kariye Camii Museum) was built between 1316 and 1321, and incorporates the shell of an earlier church. Chora means 'in the country', an allusion to an even older foundation outside the city walls. The church's patron was Metochites, who served the Emperor Andronicus II Palaelogus as prime minister and treasurer. When the emperor was overthrown in 1328, Metochites was sent into exile. Two years later he was allowed to return

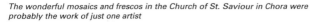
The wonderful mosaics and frescos in the Church of St. Saviour in Chora were probably the work of just one artist

as a monk to live out his days in the confines of the church he had founded.

Mosaics and frescos Fortunately, the glory of the church—its mosaics and frescos—were not destroyed when the building was converted into a mosque in 1511. They are almost certainly the work of a single unknown artist, who left his signature in the hooked tails of the drapery and the peculiar 'shadows' around the feet. The mosaics depict the life and ministry of Christ and the life of the Virgin Mary. Above the door leading into the nave is Metochites presenting his church to Christ; he is wearing the typical Byzantine sun hat known as a *skiadon*. The frescos are confined to the *parekklesion* and, as befits a mortuary chapel, depict the Last Judgement and the Harrowing of Hell.

THE BASICS

✚ b4

✉ Kariye Camii Sokağı, Edirnekapı

☎ 212-631-9241

◷ Thu–Tue 9–4.30

🍴 Cafés (€) on square; Asitane (€€€; ▷ 74)

🚫 None

✋ Moderate

❓ No flash photography

Yedikule Hisarı

Yedikule Castle (left and right) forms part of the city walls

THE BASICS

➕ Off map at a5
✉ Yedikule Meydanı
☎ 212-585-8933
🕐 Thu–Tue 9.30–4.30
🍴 Cafés (€) nearby
🚌 80
🚊 Yedikule
♿ None
💰 Inexpensive

HIGHLIGHTS

● Well of Blood
● View from the battlements
● Porta Aurea

TIP

● To explore the land walls in greater depth, follow the walk on page 73.

You could spend a whole day exploring the old Byzantine fortifications, with their watchtowers, gateways and parapets. Access is virtually unrestricted and the views are superb.

The land walls Stretching all the way from the Sea of Marmara to the Golden Horn, Constantinople's land walls enclosed the entire Byzantine city. They were built in AD412–22 during the reign of Theodosius II and, apart from severe structural damage sustained during an earthquake in 447, survived almost intact until they were finally breached in 1453 by Sultan Mehmet the Conqueror.

Yedikule Castle The Fortress of the Seven Towers assumed its present form around 1460 when Mehmet added five towers to the Porta Aurea (Golden Gate). Dating from AD390, this was originally a free-standing triumphal arch used exclusively by emperors to enter the city. The gate still exists, although the gold-plated doors and statues have long since disappeared and the arches themselves have been bricked up. First used as a treasury, the castle became a notorious place of imprisonment. In one of the towers is the cell where, in 1622, the deposed sultan, Osman II, was murdered by the traditional method of strangulation by bowstring—while simultaneously having his testicles crushed. You can also see the Well of Blood into which severed heads were unceremoniously tossed.

More to See

FATIH CAMII

Named after the conqueror of Constantinople, Sultan Fatih Mehmet, this important mosque complex actually dates from 1767. Its predecessor (built in 1463–70) was completely destroyed in an earthquake. You can see Mehmet's tomb in front of the mihrab wall.

🚩 Off map at b5 ✉ Fevzi Paşa Caddesi, Fatih ⏱ Hours of prayer 🍴 Cafés (€), restaurants (€€) nearby ♿ None 🎟 Free

HALIÇ (GOLDEN HORN)

An inlet of the Bosphorus around 8km (5 miles) in length, the Golden Horn has long provided a natural port for Istanbul. Ferries leave hourly from a pier behind Eminönü bus station, to the left of Galata Bridge. The boats criss-cross between the northern and southern shores, stopping at Fener, Balat, Hasköy, Ayvansaray and Sütlüce on their way to Eyüp (▷ 66).

🚩 d2 🚌 Eminönü

MIHRIMAH SULTAN CAMII

The patron of this beautiful mosque, Mihrimah Sultan, was the favourite daughter of Süleyman the Magnificent and the richest woman in the world at the time. She shared a passion for architecture with her husband, Rüstem Paşa, and they were patrons of Mimar Sinan, the great builder. With the Mihrimah Sultan Mosque, Sinan created a prototype for mosque design that endured throughout the Ottoman era. The focal point is the huge cuboid prayer hall, covered by a dome 36.5m (120ft) high and 20m (66ft) across. The sense of space is achieved by banishing the galleries to domed bays at the north and south ends. With this uninterrupted view, you can appreciate the magnificent decoration as you look up to the arabesque stencils between the supporting arches and across to the tiling of the mihrab wall.

🚩 a5 ✉ Ali Kuşçu Sokağı, Edirnekapı ⏱ Hours of prayer 🍴 Cafés (€) nearby 🚌 Edirnekapı ♿ None 🎟 Free

The waters of the Golden Horn

The dome and minarets of Fatih Mosque

MINIATÜRK

www.miniaturk.com.tr

Opened in 2003, this amusement park features a walk past miniature reproductions of more than 100 Turkish buildings, from palaces and mosques to airports, shopping malls and a football stadium.

⊕ Off map at d1 ⊠ Imrahor Caddesi, Sütlüce ☎ 212-222-2882 ⚙ Daily 9–5, longer hours in summer and weekends ⑪ Café (€) and restaurant (€€) 🚌 47C, 47E ⛴ Sütlüce, then short bus or *dolmuş* ride 🚶 Moderate

RAHMI M. KOÇ MÜZESI

www.rmk-museum.org.tr

Children and adults alike will enjoy this hands-on transport museum, with vintage trams, cars, boats, planes and even a submarine on display in a converted foundry beside the Golden Horn.

⊕ e1 ⊠ Hasköy Caddesi 27, Hasköy ☎ 212-369-6600 ⚙ Tue–Fri 10–5, Sat, Sun 10–7 ⑪ Café (€) and restaurants (€€; ▷ 74) ⛴ Sütlüce 🚻 Good 🚶 Moderate

RUM PATRIKHANESI (ECUMENICAL ORTHODOX PATRIARCHATE)

The district of Fener is the traditional home of Istanbul's Greek community and the worldwide home of the Eastern Orthodox church, which continued to be based in Constantinople even after the Ottoman conquest. As the ecumenical patriarch of the Orthodox communion, the Archbishop of Constantinople and New Rome is the spiritual leader of 250 million Christians in Russia, Greece and elsewhere. His seat, the cathedral of St. George, was completed in 1720 as a three-aisled basilica with a carved wood iconostasis separating the sanctuary from the nave. The Divine Liturgy is held here every Sunday morning and the church is the focus for Orthodox celebrations at Easter.

⊕ e5 ⊠ Sadrazam Ali Paşa Caddesi, Fener ☎ 212-531-9670 ⚙ Daily 9–5 ⛴ Fener 🚶 Free/donation

Lighting candles in the Ecumenical Orthodox Patriarchate

Exploring the Land Walls

Take a walk in the shadow of the fifth-century Byzantine walls, which protected the city for a thousand years.

DISTANCE: 2.5km (1.5 miles) **ALLOW:** 1 hour

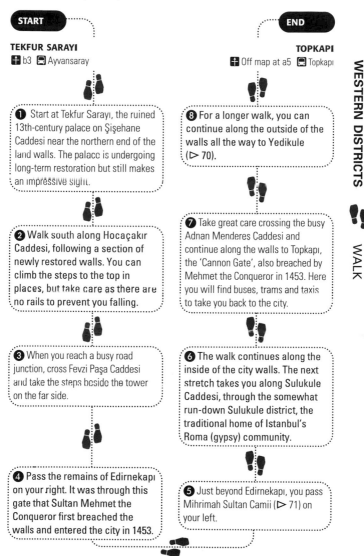

START

TEKFUR SARAYI
✚ b3 🚇 Ayvansaray

❶ Start at Tekfur Sarayı, the ruined 13th-century palace on Şişehane Caddesi near the northern end of the land walls. The palace is undergoing long-term restoration but still makes an impressive sight.

❷ Walk south along Hocaçakır Caddesi, following a section of newly restored walls. You can climb the steps to the top in places, but take care as there are no rails to prevent you falling.

❸ When you reach a busy road junction, cross Fevzi Paşa Caddesi and take the steps beside the tower on the far side.

❹ Pass the remains of Edirnekapı on your right. It was through this gate that Sultan Mehmet the Conqueror first breached the walls and entered the city in 1453.

END

TOPKAPI
✚ Off map at a5 🚇 Topkapı

❽ For a longer walk, you can continue along the outside of the walls all the way to Yedikule (▷ 70).

❼ Take great care crossing the busy Adnan Menderes Caddesi and continue along the walls to Topkapı, the 'Cannon Gate', also breached by Mehmet the Conqueror in 1453. Here you will find buses, trams and taxis to take you back to the city.

❻ The walk continues along the inside of the city walls. The next stretch takes you along Sulukule Caddesi, through the somewhat run-down Sulukule district, the traditional home of Istanbul's Roma (gypsy) community.

❺ Just beyond Edirnekapı, you pass Mihrimah Sultan Camii (▷ 71) on your left.

Restaurants

PRICES

Prices are approximate, based on a three-course meal for one person.

€€€   more than 40 YTL
€€   20–40 YTL
€   under 20 YTL

ASITANE (€€€)

This hotel restaurant beside Kariye Camii re-creates authentic Ottoman recipes, including several served at a circumcision feast in 1539 for Süleyman the Magnificent's sons. How about almond and coconut soup followed by melon stuffed with mincemeat, rice, almonds, currants and pistachios? In summer you can dine in the pretty garden.

🚉 b5 ✉ Kariye Camii Sokağı 18, Edirnekapı ☎ 212-635-7997 🕐 Daily 11–10.30 🚇 Edirnekapı

CAFÉ DU LEVANT (€€)

This is one of two restaurants belonging to the Rahmi M. Koç Museum (▷ 72), both of which offer alternatives to the standard repertoire of Turkish cuisine. The aim of Café du Levant is to re-create an authentic Parisian brasserie on the streets of Istanbul. The decor reflects this, with stained glass, tiled floors, wooden tables and French posters on the walls, while the menu features classic French dishes and wines.

🚉 e1 ✉ Hasköy Caddesi 27, Hasköy ☎ 212-369-6607 🕐 Tue–Sun 10–10 🚇 Hasköy

DEVELI (€€

Established in 1912, this popular restaurant in Samatya serves the best kebabs in town, including aubergine (eggplant), pistachio, yoghurt and garlic kebabs, as well as an excellent selection of *mezes*, salads and *pide* bread. Ask for a table on the fifth-floor terrace

MEZES

In a typical Istanbul restaurant, you will be offered a selection of hot and cold appetizers known collectively as *mezes*. They range from simple salads dressed in olive oil to aubergine (eggplant) purée and Çengelköy cucumbers, and from *biber dolması* (green peppers stuffed with raisins, rice and pine nuts) to fried *kalamar* with *tarator* (breadcrumbs flavoured with garlic and walnut), Albanian diced liver and pastries seasoned with fresh herbs. *Mezes* are usually accompanied by fresh white bread.

with views over the Sea of Marmara.

🚉 Off map at A12 ✉ Gümüşyüzük Sokağı 7 ☎ 212-529-0833 🕐 Daily 12–12 🚇 Koca Mustafa Paşa

HALAT (€€€)

The main restaurant at the Rahmi M. Koç Museum (▷ 72) offers sophisticated Mediterranean seafood dishes in a maritime setting, and it has a charming waterfront terrace beside the Golden Horn. During the day it is open for sandwiches and light snacks, but the best time to come is on a summer evening, when the twinkling lights of Istanbul are reflected in the water and the call to prayer drifts across from the mosques of Fener and Balat.

🚉 e1 ✉ Hasköy Caddesi 27, Hasköy ☎ 212-369-6616 🕐 Tue–Sun 10–10 🚇 Hasköy

KARIYE PEMBE KÖŞK (€€)

With tables on a pretty square facing Kariye Camii and a simple menu of toasted sandwiches, kebabs and lentil soup, this makes a good choice for a quick lunch after visiting the museum.

🚉 b4 ✉ Kariye Camii Sokağı 27 ☎ 212-635-8586 🕐 Daily 9am–11pm 🚇 Edirnekapı

Cross the Galata Bridge from Eminönü and you leave old Istanbul behind. This is Beyoğlu, the 19th-century European quarter north of the Golden Horn, whose central boulevard, Istiklal Caddesi, buzzes with activity day and night.

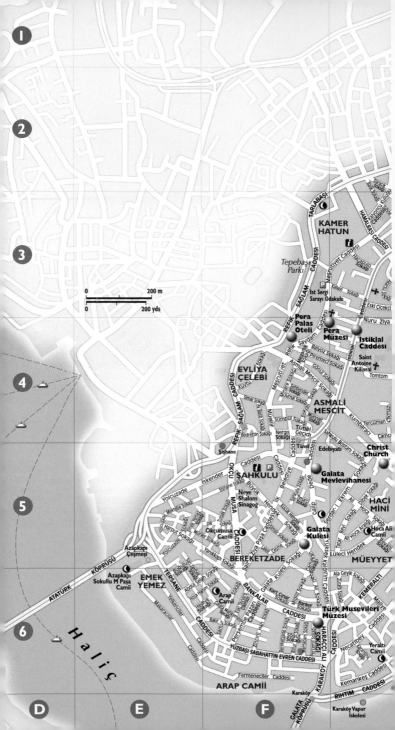

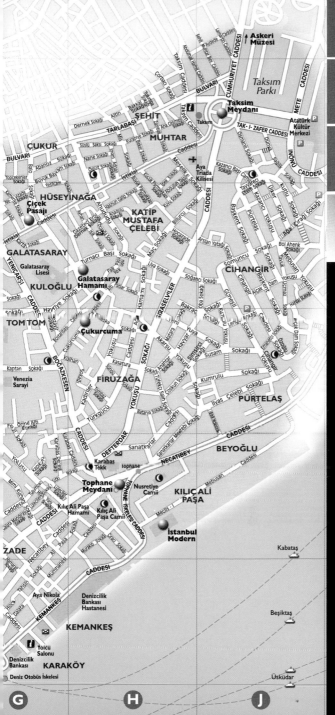

Istanbul Modern

HIGHLIGHTS

● *Han Coffee House* by Bedri Rahmi Eyüboğlu
● *Music Shop at Tünel* by Muhçin Kut
● *Kapı (Door)* by Burhan Uygur
● *Stairway to Hell* by Monica Bonvicini

TIP

● Visit the museum on a Thursday, when there is free admission and extended opening hours.

With contemporary Turkish and international art housed in a dramatic waterfront setting, this modern art museum aims to put Istanbul on the European cultural map, alongside London, Paris and Barcelona.

The building Istanbul Modern opened in December 2004 in a former customs warehouse on the pier at Karaköy. The lower floor is given over to temporary exhibitions and a photography gallery, cinema and new media room, while the permanent exhibition is upstairs in the main hall. With its sleek white walls and picture windows giving views across the Bosphorus to Topkapı Palace, it makes a stunning setting for a display of 20th-century Turkish art.

Istanbul Modern, in a former customs warehouse, displays contemporary art

The collection The items in the permanent collection are rotated annually but are mostly arranged by themes such as landscapes, city life, self-portraits and abstract art. In addition, there are entire galleries dedicated to individual Turkish painters, including Ihsan Cemal Karaburçak (1897–1970), an abstract artist who took up painting only at the age of 33. You cannot miss *Stairway to Hell*, by Venetian artist Monica Bonvicini, a tortured structure of steel chains and broken glass that stands at the heart of the main hall, acting both as a piece of installation art and as the staircase between upper and lower galleries.

Light relief When you need a break, the museum café has a delightful terrace beside the Bosphorus.

THE BASICS

www.istanbulmodern.org
✚ H5
✉ Meclis-i Mebusan Caddesi, Karaköy
☎ 212-334-7300
🕐 Tue, Wed, Fri–Sun 10–6, Thu 10–8
🍴 Café and restaurant (€€)
🚇 Tophane
♿ Fully accessible
💰 Moderate (free on Thu)
❓ Free guided tours at 1 and 3 daily

Istiklal Caddesi

new town

TOP 25

HIGHLIGHTS

- Tünel funicular and tram
- Galatasaray Lycée
- Church of St. Mary Draperis
- Church of St. Anthony of Padua
- Çiçek Pasajı (▷ 82)

TIP

● Take the old-fashioned funicular from Karaköy to Tünel, walk along Istiklal Caddesi, then take the modern funicular from Taksim to Kabataş to return to Karaköy by tram.

Independence Avenue is Istanbul's most popular promenade and the focus of evening entertainment. A nostalgic tram journey takes you the entire length of the pedestrianized shopping street, from Tünel to Taksim Square.

Grande Rue de Pera In the 19th century, this was the Grande Rue de Pera, the central thoroughfare of Istanbul's European quarter. Most of the foreign embassies were located here, along with churches, grand apartment blocks and fashionable hotels. Visitors arriving on the Orient Express and taking the funicular to Tünel christened Istanbul 'the Paris of the East'. But after the Turkish capital moved to Ankara in 1923, the ambassadors moved out and Pera went into decline.

Istiklal Caddesi is the place to be seen in Istanbul

A street for strolling Today, Istiklal Caddesi has recovered its former cachet and is once again the place to be seen in Istanbul. Music blares out of cafés day and night, and the street is lined with bookstores, cinemas, art galleries and clothes shops. Pedestrianization has given the area a new lease of life; on weekend afternoons, half of Istanbul seems to be strolling here and showing off the latest fashions.

Vintage tram If you don't want to walk, take the antique tram that rattles up and down between Tünel and Taksim Square, pausing halfway outside the 19th-century Galatasaray Lycée. The trams stopped service in 1961 but were reintroduced 30 years later during a wave of nostalgia.

> **THE BASICS**
>
> ➕ G4
> 🍽 Lots of cafés (€) and restaurants (€€) in nearby streets
> Ⓜ Funicular to Tünel or Taksim
> 🚌 Taksim

More to See

ASKERI MÜZESI

Walk up Cumhuriyet Caddesi from Taksim Square to reach the Military Museum, with its vast collection of Ottoman and Turkish weapons, uniforms and flags. Arrive before 3pm for the daily concert by the Mehter military orchestra, a marching band resplendent in red Ottoman uniforms with clashing cymbals, pipes and drums.

➕ Off map at J1 ✉ Vali Konaği Caddesi, Harbiye ☎ 212-233-2720 ⏰ Wed–Sun 9–4.30 🚇 Osmanbey ✋ Inexpensive

CHRIST CHURCH

This Victorian Gothic Revival church, designed by GE Street, who was the architect of the Royal Courts of Justice in London, was established in 1858 by decree of Sultan Abdulmecit for the English population of Istanbul. It is now the parish church of the city's Anglican community.

➕ G5 ✉ Serdar-i Ekrem Sokak 82, Tünel ☎ 212-251-5616 ⏰ Holy Communion: Sun 10am 🚇 Funicular to Tünel

ÇIÇEK PASAJI

An elegant 19th-century shopping arcade off Istiklal Caddesi (▷ 80), the Çiçek Pasajı (Flower Passage) now houses several *meyhanes* (▷ 88) where gypsy musicians perform most nights. The adjoining street, Sahne Sokağı, is known as the Balık Pazarı (Fish Market).

➕ G3 🚇 Taksim; funicular to Tünel 🚇 Taksim

ÇUKURCUMA

The steeply sloping streets behind Galatasaray Lycée lead to this attractive residential district, home to Istanbul's largest concentration of antiques shops. The best places for browsing are along Faik Paşa Yokuşu and Çukurcuma Caddesi.

➕ H4 🚇 Taksim 🚇 Funicular to Tünel

GALATA KULESI

A steep climb up Galata Kulesi Sokağı or a short walk downhill from Tünel leads to the round Galata Tower, built as a Genoese fortification in 1348 and later used

A night scene in Çiçek Pasajı

as a barracks, prison and astronomical observatory. Take the lift to the viewing platform for sunset views. At night, the tower is used for belly-dancing shows (▷ 87).

➕ F5 ✉ Galata Meydanı, Tünel ☎ 212-293-8180 ⏰ Daily 9–8 🚇 Funicular to Tünel 💷 Moderate

GALATA MEVLEVIHANESI

This *tekke* (dervish lodge) was closed in the 1920s but is now the Museum of Classical Literature. The tomb of 17th-century Sufi poet Galip Dede stands in the garden. The main reason to come here is to see the mystical whirling dervish ceremony (▷ 86, 87).

➕ F5 ✉ Galip Dede Caddesi 15, Tünel ☎ 212-245-4141 ⏰ Wed–Mon 9.30–4.30 🚇 Funicular to Tünel 💷 Inexpensive

GALATASARAY HAMAMI

These 15th-century baths, built by Sultan Beyazıt II, were restored in the 1960s with the addition of a women's section. Heated by natural gas, the *hararet* (steam room) is probably the hottest in Istanbul.

➕ H3 ✉ Turnacıbaşı Sokağı 24, Galatasaray ☎ 212-249-4342 ⏰ Daily 6am–10pm for men; daily 8–8 for women 🚇 Taksim; funicular to Tünel 🚇 Taksim

PERA MÜZESI

www.peramuzesi.org.tr

This excellent private museum opened in 2005 in the former Hotel Bristol, built in 1893 during the grand old days of Pera. The permanent exhibition, displayed over two floors, features an eclectic collection of Anatolian weights and measures, Kütahya ceramics and Ottoman-era portraits by European Orientalist painters. Look for *The Tortoise Trainer*, the best-known work by Turkish archaeologist and artist Osman Hamdi Bey (1842–1910).

➕ G4 ✉ Meşrutiyet Caddesi 141, Tepebaşı ☎ 212-334-9900 ⏰ Tue–Sat 10–7, Sun 12–6 🍴 Café (€) ♿ Good 💷 Moderate 🚇 Funicular to Tünel

You can see whirling dervishes at Galata Mevlevihanesi

The Galata Tower, from across the Bosphorus

★

PERA PALAS OTELI

The grande dame of Istanbul hotels opened in 1892 for passengers arriving on the Orient Express. Among the guests was crime writer Agatha Christie, who stayed in Room 411 while writing *Murder on the Orient Express*. Before it closed for renovation in 2006, the hotel had a time-warp museum feel, with staff taking visitors up in the birdcage lift to see Christie's room and the room used by Kemal Atatürk. The Pera Palace is expected to reopen by late 2008 (▷ 112).

🔟 F4 ✉ Meşrutiyet Caddesi 98–100, Tepebaşı 🔘 Funicular to Tünel

TAKSIM MEYDANI

This vast, traffic choked square at the top of Istiklal Caddesi (▷ 80–81) takes its name from the stone reservoir on its western side. At its heart is the Cumhuriyet (Republic) Monument, designed by Italian sculptor Pietro Canonica in 1928 and depicting Atatürk

and other revolutionary leaders.
🔟 J2 🔘 Taksim 🚋 Taksim

TOPHANE MEYDANI

Hidden at the back of a small park behind Nusretiye Mosque, in the shadow of an old cannon foundry built under Mehmet the Conqueror, is a row of cafés that are crowded day and night with people smoking *nargiles* (▷ 86). It's a good place to relax after a visit to Istanbul Modern (▷ 78–79).
🔟 H5 🚋 Tophane

TÜRK MUSEVILERI MÜZESI

Housed in the 19th-century Zulfaris synagogue, the Jewish Museum tells the story of five centuries of Jewish life in Istanbul, from the arrival of the first Sephardic Jews in 1492, welcomed by Sultan Beyazıt II after their expulsion from Spain.
🔟 F6 ✉ Perçemli Sokağı, Karaköy ☎ 212-292-6333 🕐 Mon–Thu 10–4, Fri, Sun 10–2 🚋 Karaköy 🚫 None 🖐 Moderate

Republic Monument, in Taksim Square   *An old water tower in Tophane Park*

Shopping

ANTIKARNAS
You'll find a wide range of Ottoman antiques and curios on sale at this restored four-floor town house in Çukurcuma, as well as various Turkish and European items.
⊞ H3 ⊠ Faik Paşa Yokuşu 15, Çukurcuma ☎ 212-251 5928 ⊚ Taksim 🚋 Taksim

GALERI ALFA
On the main antiques street of Çukurcuma, this shop sells old maps and prints as well as Ottoman toy soldiers.
⊞ H3 ⊠ Faik Paşa Yokuşu 47, Çukurcuma ☎ 212-251-1672 ⊚ Taksim 🚋 Taksim

GÖNÜL PAKSOY
This brilliant young designer is at the cutting edge of Ottoman chic, turning scarves, shawls, slippers and jewellery into works of art through the use of natural fabrics and traditional Ottoman designs.
⊞ Off map at J1 ⊠ Atiye Sokağı 6/A, Teşvikiye ☎ 212-236-0209 🚋 Teşvikiye

HOMER
www.homerbooks.com
Turkey's biggest publisher of English-language books has a small shop in Galatasaray selling its own and other titles.
⊞ G3 ⊠ Yeni Çarşı Caddesi 12/A, Galatasaray, Beyoğlu ☎ 212-249-5902 ⊚ Funicular to Tünel

ISTANBUL MÜZIK MERKEZI
This is one of many shops selling musical instruments along Galip Dede Caddesi, a street running down from the Tünel funicular station.
⊞ F5 ⊠ Galip Dede Caddesi 21, Tünel ☎ 212-244-5885 ⊚ Funicular to Tünel

MAVI JEANS
This popular store is where the city's young and trendy come to get their jeans, as well as denim skirts, T-shirts and accessories.
⊞ H2 ⊠ Istiklal Caddesi 123, Beyoğlu ☎ 212-244-6255 ⊚ Taksim 🚋 Taksim

MEGAVIZYON
This multimedia megastore has everything from CDs to computer software and books. Lots of other shops

ANTIQUES GALORE

Istanbul probably has more antiques shops per square kilometre than any other European city, selling everything from Ottoman furniture to candlesticks. There are at least 85 shops packed into the narrow streets of the Çukurcuma district alone. Alternatively, take the boat to the Sunday market on Ortaköy waterfront, where local artists sell handicrafts and paintings.

along Istiklal Caddesi sell music, and the latest hits blare out late into the evening.
⊞ H2 ⊠ Istiklal Caddesi 57B, Beyoğlu ☎ 212-293-0759 ⊚ Taksim 🚋 Taksim

OTTOMAN EMPIRE
Contemporary chic meets traditional Turkish art at this funky boutique in Teşvikiye, which sells T-shirts inspired by Ottoman calligraphy and designs.
⊞ Off map at J1 ⊠ Şakayik Sokağı 59/1, Teşvikiye ☎ 212-296-5619 🚋 Teşvikiye

OTTOMANIA
Antique books, maps and prints from one of the most respected dealers in Istanbul.
⊞ F4 ⊠ Sofyalı Sokağı 30–32, Tünel ☎ 212-243-2157 ⊚ Funicular to Tünel

PAŞABAHÇE
Turkey's leading glassware manufacturer also owns a retail chain whose biggest branch is on Istiklal Caddesi.
⊞ G4 ⊠ Istiklal Caddesi 314, Beyoğlu ☎ 212-244 0544 ⊚ Funicular to Tünel

ROBINSON CRUSOE
A huge bookshop with a good range of English-language titles.
⊞ G4 ⊠ Istiklal Caddesi 389, Beyoğlu ☎ 212-293-6968 ⊚ Mon–Sat 9am–9.30pm, Sun 10 9.30 ⊚ Funicular to Tünel

BEYOĞLU

SHOPPING

Entertainment and Nightlife

360

This modern Turkish restaurant on the top floor of a 19th-century apartment block turns into an ultra-trendy bar at night, where a hip crowd sips cocktails on a rooftop terrace with 360-degree views.
➕ G3 ✉ Istiklal Caddesi 309, Beyoğlu ☎ 212-251-1042 ⏰ Daily 6pm–3am 🚠 Funicular to Tünel

AKBANK SANAT

www.akbanksanat.com
This popular venue for classical music, jazz concerts and films hosts the Akbank Jazz Festival in October.
➕ H2 ✉ Istiklal Caddesi 14–18, Beyoğlu ☎ 212-252-3500 🚇 Taksim 🚇 Taksim

ATATÜRK KÜLTÜR MERKEZI

With five concert halls, an art gallery and a cinema, this is the largest and most important arts complex in Istanbul. There are regular performances by the Istanbul Symphony Orchestra and the city's opera, ballet and drama companies, as well as by visiting companies from abroad. AKM is also a major venue during the Istanbul International Music Festival in June and July. For information on current productions, call in at the booking office at the front of the venue.

➕ J2 ✉ Taksim Meydanı, Beyoğlu ☎ 212-251-5600 ⏰ Box office daily 10–6 🚇 Taksim 🚇 Taksim

BABYLON

www.babylon.com.tr
Istanbul's premier venue for live rock, jazz and world music, including big-name international stars. In July and August it opens only for occasional special events, as the clubbing scene moves out-of-doors to the Bosphorus shore.
➕ F4 ✉ Şehbender Sokağı 3, Tünel ☎ 212-292-7368

NARGILES

Once the preserve of wizened old men in cafés, the *nargile* (water-cooled tobacco pipe) has seen a revival in recent years and fashionable young people now puff away at these strange contraptions, with their glass bottles, metal pipes, detachable mouthpieces and glowing coals. Most people opt for apple-scented tobacco but some places offer everything from pistachio to cappuccino. Various *nargile* joints have sprung up behind the Nusretiye Mosque, at Tophane, where Istanbul's bright young things smoke hookahs and lounge on cushions late into the night.

⏰ Tue–Sat 9.30pm–2am; box office 12–9 🚠 Funicular to Tünel

BADEHANE

This busy bar near the Tünel funicular spills out onto the street in summer. It makes a good place for a drink at any time, but the atmosphere is liveliest on Wednesday evening, when gypsy musicians often play here.
➕ F4 ✉ General Yazgan Sokağı 5, Tünel ☎ 212-249-0550 ⏰ Daily 9am–2am 🚠 Funicular to Tünel

CEMAL REŞIT REY KONSER SALONU

An attractive concert hall used for recitals of classical and Ottoman chamber music.
➕ Off map at J1 ✉ Gümüş Sokağı, Harbiye ☎ 212-232-9830 ⏰ Box office daily 10–7.30 🚌 Harbiye

GALATA MEVLEVIHANESI

This Sufi monastery and dervish lodge near the Galata Tower is the best place to see the mystical whirling dervish ceremony known as the *Sema*, which is usually held on alternate Sunday afternoons. Tickets are limited and sell quickly, so buy them from the monastery in advance.
➕ F5 ✉ Galip Dede Caddesi 15, Tünel ☎ 212-245-4141 ⏰ Sun 5pm 🚠 Funicular to Tünel

GALATASARAY HAMAMI
See page 83.

GALATA TOWER
www.galatatower.net
On the ninth floor of one of Istanbul's most famous landmarks, there are great views of the city by night as you watch the cabaret and belly-dancing show.
F5 ⊠ Galata Meydanı, Tünel ☎ 212-293-8180 ⊙ Mon–Sat 8pm–midnight ⊜ Funicular to Tünel

KERVANSARAY
Expensive and theatrical, the dinner show has a live orchestra and voluptuous belly-dancers, plus the chance to have your photo taken dressed as an Ottoman sultan or sultana. Ask for a free shuttle from your hotel when you book.
Off map at J1 ⊠ Cumhuriyet Caddesi 30, Harbiye ☎ 212-247-1630 ⊙ Daily 7.30pm ⊜ Taksim ⊟ Taksim

KEVE
Classy bar-café in a 19th-century arcade opposite the upper exit of the Tünel funicular, among old-fashioned street lamps and potted plants—a great place for an early-evening or late-night drink.
F4 ⊠ Tünel Geçidi 10, Tünel ☎ 212-251-4338 ⊙ Daily 8am–2am ⊜ Funicular to Tünel

MUNZUR
Munzur is one of a handful of late-night bars along Hasnün Galip Sokağı specializing in Anatolian folk music, with an emphasis on the *bağlama* or *saz* (mandolin). There is no admission charge but tips are expected and drinks are more expensive than elsewhere.
H3 ⊠ Hasnün Galip Sokağı 21A, Beyoğlu ☎ 212-245-4669 ⊙ Daily 6pm–3am ⊜ Taksim ⊟ Taksim

NARDIS
www.nardisjazz.com
In a medieval cellar near to the Galata Tower,

WHIRLING DERVISHES

The Sufi tradition of whirling dervishes, in which dancers reach a state of spiritual ecstasy through trance-like music and movement, originated in the Turkish city of Konya in the 13th century. The whirling usually takes place during the mystical *Sema* ceremony, accompanied by chanting and music on the reed flute, zither and drums. The best place to see it is at Galata Mevlevihanesi (▷ 86). Although it has become a popular tourist attraction, it is important to remember that this is primarily a religious ceremony.

Nardis is a cool, smoky jazz club.
F5 ⊠ Galata Kulesi Sokağı 14, Tünel ☎ 212-244-6327 ⊙ Mon–Thu 9pm–1am, Fri, Sat 10pm–2am ⊜ Funicular to Tünel

NARGILEM
One of a long row of places serving tea and *nargiles* to a late-night crowd behind the Nusretiye Mosque in Tophane.
H5 ⊠ Necatibey Caddesi, Tophane ☎ 212-244-2492 ⊙ Daily 24 hours ⊟ Tophane

ROXY
The only serious rival to Babylon (▷ 86) as a live music venue, attracting a young crowd with its hip-hop electronic and dance music. Closed from July to September.
J3 ⊠ Arslan Yatağı Sokağı 7, Beyoğlu ☎ 212-249-1283 ⊙ Wed–Sat 10pm–4am ⊜ Taksim ⊟ Taksim

TÜRKÜ
Many of the bars in the side streets off the top end of Istiklal Caddesi have live folk and pop music each night. This small bar is a good place to hear authentic folk instruments such as the *saz* (the Turkish mandolin).
H2 ⊠ Imam Adnan Sokağı 9, Beyoğlu ☎ 212-292-9281 ⊙ Daily noon–2am ⊜ Taksim ⊟ Taksim

BEYOĞLU

ENTERTAINMENT AND NIGHTLIFE

Restaurants

PRICES

Prices are approximate, based on a three-course meal for one person.

€€€	over 40 YTL
€€	20–40 YTL
€	under 20 YTL

ASMALIMESCIT BALIKÇISI (€€)

On a busy *meyhane* strip near Tünel station, this well-known fish restaurant features live music, regular art exhibitions and a wide-ranging menu of grilled fish, seafood and fishy *mezes*.

✚ F4 ✉ Sofyalı Sokağı 5, Tünel ☎ 212-251-3939 ◷ Mon–Fri 12–2, 6–12, Sat, Sun 6–12 Ⓠ Funicular to Tünel

BONCUK (€€)

Enjoy delicious Armenian and Turkish *mezes*, including aubergine (eggplant) purée, cucumber with yoghurt, and samphire in lemon and olive oil, all washed down with *rakı* at tables on the street.

✚ G3 ✉ Nevizade Sokağı 19, Galatarasay ☎ 212-243-1219 ◷ Daily 12–12 Ⓠ Taksim ▣ Taksim

GALATA EVI (€€)

In a former jail below the Galata Tower, this unusual restaurant has been converted by a husband-and-wife team of architects, and now serves Russian and Georgian cuisine, such as beetroot soup, lamb stew with plums, goulash and potato dumplings.

✚ F6 ✉ Galata Kulesi Sokağı 61, Tünel ☎ 212-245-1861 ◷ Tue–Sun 12–12 Ⓠ Funicular to Tünel

HACI ABDULLAH (€€)

The oldest and best of Istanbul's *lokantas*, offering ready-prepared dishes such as *imam bayildi* and stuffed vegetables, plus grilled meat and kebabs in a side street off Istiklal Caddesi. No alcohol.

✚ H2 ✉ Sakızağacı

MEYHANES

A *meyhane* is a tavern where people go to eat *mezes*, invariably washed down by large amounts of *rakı*. Waiters dash around bearing huge trays of *mezes* from which diners make their choice. Although most *meyhanes* also serve grilled meat and fish, it is quite normal to order enough appetizers for everyone to share and skip the main course. These places are particularly good for vegetarians. The liveliest *meyhanes* are in Beyoğlu, on Sofyalı Sokağı near the Tünel funicular and Nevizade Sokağı, half-way up Istiklal Caddesi.

Caddesi 17, Beyoğlu ☎ 212-293-8561 ◷ Daily 12–10.30 Ⓠ Taksim ▣ Taksim

IMROZ (€€)

One of the most popular places along the busiest restaurant strip in town, Imroz heaves with diners tucking into platters of *mezes* and grilled fish on weekend evenings.

✚ G3 ✉ Nevizade Sokağı 24, Galatarasay ☎ 212-249-9073 ◷ Daily 12–12 Ⓠ Taksim ▣ Taksim

LOKANTA (€€€)

Enjoy funky Turkish-Mediterranean fusion cuisine in a Manhattan-style loft space with exposed brick walls. In summer the restaurant moves upstairs to the Nu Teras rooftop terrace.

✚ F4 ✉ Meşrutiyet Caddesi 149, Tepebaşı ☎ 212-245-6070 ◷ Daily 12–3, 7–12 Ⓠ Funicular to Tünel

MADO (€)

This popular chain outlet sells the best ice cream in Istanbul, made from 100 per cent goat's milk with varieties that include cream, chocolate, pistachio and sour cherry. The biggest branch is on Istiklal Caddesi, and there is another by the port at Ortaköy.

✚ G3 ✉ Istiklal Caddesi 88, Beyoğlu ☎ 212-244-1781 ◷ Daily 9am–1am Ⓠ Funicular to Tünel

MIKLA (€€€)

On the top floors of the Marmara Pera Hotel, Mikla is the latest project of Turko-Finnish chef Mehmet Gürs, who is pushing back the boundaries of modern Turkish cuisine with new-wave Mediterranean and Scandinavian creations. In summer, there are outdoor terraces and a cool rooftop cocktail bar and pool.

➕ F4 ✉ Meşrutiyet Caddesi 167–185, Tepebaşı ☎ 212-293-5656 ⏱ Daily noon–2am 🚇 Funicular to Tünel

NATURE & PEACE (€)

Istanbul's oldest vegetarian restaurant offers soups, salads, pasta and lentil dishes, as well as a daily set menu and a handful of meat dishes.

➕ H3 ✉ Büyükparmakkapı Sokağı 21, Beyoğlu ☎ 212-252-8609 ⏱ Daily 12–12 🚇 Taksim 🚊 Taksim

NEYLE MEYLE (€€)

Seafood, grilled fish and vegetarian *mezes* are all on the menu at this lively *meyhane*.

➕ G3 ✉ Nevizade Sokağı 12, Galatarasay ☎ 212-249-8103 ⏱ Daily 12–12 🚇 Taksim 🚊 Taksim

OTANTIK (€)

Women in Anatolian costume make *gözleme* (pancakes) in the window of this rustic restaurant, which serves cheap, filling Anatolian

dishes such as potato dumplings, casseroles and pancakes.

➕ G3 ✉ Istiklal Caddesi 80, Beyoğlu ☎ 212-293-8451 ⏱ Daily 9am–10pm 🚇 Funicular to Tünel

PALMIYE (€€)

In the famous 'Flower Passage' (Çiçek Pasaji, ▷ 82), Palmiye offers *mezes*, meat and fish dishes.

➕ G3 ✉ Çiçek Pasaji, Galatasaray ☎ 212-249-2101 ⏱ Daily 11am–midnight 🚇 Taksim 🚊 Taksim

PATISSERIE MARKIZ (€)

The art nouveau interior and rich cakes and pastries conjure up the atmosphere of the Grande Rue de Pera

---

RAKI

The national drink of Turkey, *rakı*, is distilled from sweet raisins, with anise added. The word derives from the Arabic *araki* ('sweating'), a reference to the distilling process. Most Turks drink *rakı* mixed with ice and water, which turns it a milky hue—it is referred to colloquially as the 'lion's milk'. *Rakı* production became a state monopoly in the 1930s and it was privatized only in 2004. The most popular variety of the drink, Yeni Rakı, is 45 per cent proof.

(▷ 80) at this wonderfully decadent 19th-century café on Istiklal Caddesi. Reopened in 2003 after an absence of 23 years, it was sold to a Finnish chain in 2007 and is now a branch of Robert's Coffee.

➕ G4 ✉ Istiklal Caddesi 172, Beyoğlu ☎ 212-252-2701 ⏱ Daily 8am–midnight 🚇 Funicular to Tünel

REFIK (€€)

The oldest of the *meyhanes* in the Tünel district features mostly fish dishes, as well as *mezes* and salads.

➕ F4 ✉ Sofyalı Sokağı 10, Tünel ☎ 212-243-2834 ⏱ Mon–Sat 12–12, Sun 6pm–midnight 🚇 Funicular to Tünel

SOFYALI 9 (€€)

This busy tavern offers *mezes* and grills in a lovely old house in Tünel. Arrive early or come late if you want a table out on the street.

➕ F4 ✉ Sofyalı Sokağı 9, Tünel ☎ 212-245-0362 ⏱ Mon–Sat 12–12 🚇 Funicular to Tünel

VENTA DEL TORO (€€)

Spanish-style tapas bar beside the Galata Tower offering paella, tortilla, ham and other Spanish classics as well as 'Turkish tapas'.

➕ F5 ✉ Galip Dede Caddesi 145, Tünel ☎ 212-243-6049 ⏱ Daily 11am–2am 🚇 Funicular to Tünel

You can't fully experience Istanbul without taking to the water, on ferries that cross the Bosphorus between the Asian and European shores, passing decadent Ottoman palaces built by the sultans during the dying days of empire.

Farther Afield

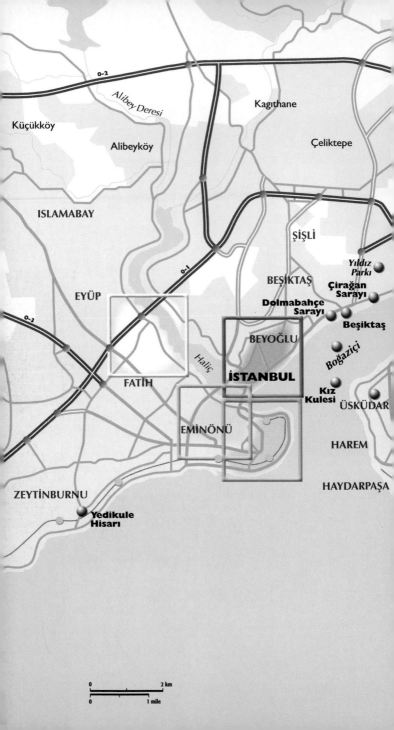

İstinye

Sadberk
Hanim Müzesi

Anadolu
Kavağı

Çubuklu

Kanlıca

Rumeli
Hisarı

Anadolu
Hisarı

Levent

Bebek

Küçüksu
Kasrı

Göksu Deresi

Arnavutköy

Kandilli

Vaniköy

Çengelköy

Ortaköy /
Ortaköy Camii

BEYLERBEYİ

Beylerbeyi
Sarayı

Büyük
Çamlıca

O-1

Bulgurlu

Ümraniye

KADMODA

Kadıköy

KIZILTOPRAK

FENERBAHÇE

İstanbul
Oyuncak
Müzesi

ERENKÖY

Fener Burun

Bostancı

Beylerbeyi Sarayı

Exterior view (left);
a chandelier and
ornate decoration
inside (right)

THE BASICS

➕ Off map to east
✉ Abdullah Ağa Caddesi
☎ 216-321-9320
🕐 Tue, Wed, Fri–Sun
9.30–4
🍴 Café (€)
🚌 15 from Üsküdar
♿ None
💵 Moderate
❓ Guided tours only.
Extra charge for
photography

HIGHLIGHTS

● Empress Eugénie's room
● Bronze horse in grounds
● Terrace garden
● Harem waterfront gate
● Rush-matting floors
● Rope motif furniture in
Admiral's Sitting Room
● Pool salon
● Wooden staircase link-
ing *harem* with *selamlık*
● Blue reception room
● Wood panels
● Prayer room with rugs
● Abdülaziz's reinforced
bed

You arrive at Beylerbeyi Palace to the beguiling sounds of Asian music, transmitted through speakers concealed among the magnolias of the terrace garden. Before the guided tour begins, admire the views across to Ortaköy.

French empress This attractive summer palace was built for Sultan Abdülaziz in 1861. Its most celebrated occupant was Empress Eugénie of France, wife of Napoleon III, who stayed here in 1869 en route to opening the Suez Canal. Abdülaziz is said to have become infatuated with her after attending the Paris exhibition two years earlier, and went to immense trouble to make her visit enjoyable.

The palace Comprising just 24 rooms and 6 salons, divided into the traditional *selamlık* and *harem*, Beylerbeyi is more modest, though no less luxurious than Dolmabahçe (▷ 96–97). To keep the apartments cool in summer, all the floors were covered with rush mats, and a recessed marble pool and fountain were built into the floor of the Pool Salon—one of the most impressive rooms in the palace. Abdülaziz was a keen sailor, and in the Admiral's Sitting Room all the furniture is ingeniously carved with rope motifs. Visitors are also shown Empress Eugénie's suite, with its specially Westernized bathroom, the Sultan's prayer room and the 2m-long (6.5ft) bed reinforced to accommodate his enormous frame—he was a formidable wrestler!

A boat trip on the Bosphorus should be on every visitor's must-do list

Boğaziçi (Bosphorus)

One of Istanbul's most unforgettable experiences is to sail out onto the Bosphorus, passing fishing villages, medieval fortresses, sumptuous Ottoman palaces and shuttered _yalıs_ (wooden mansions).

Ford of the ox The Bosphorus is a narrow stretch of water about 30km (18.5 miles) long which threads its way from the Sea of Marmara to the Black Sea, forming a natural barrier between Europe and Asia. Bosphorus means 'ford of the ox' and derives from the Greek myth of Io. While being hotly pursued by Hera, wife of Zeus, Io is turned into an ox and in that guise escapes across the strait. Today the Bosphorus is spanned by two road bridges.

Ports of call The cheapest way to see the Bosphorus is to take the ferry—there are daily departures from the pier at Eminönü, beside the Galata Bridge. There are several stops en route. Kanlıca is famous for its yoghurt, served with jam, sugar or honey in the square behind the pier. Yeniköy has splendid art nouveau mansions lining the waterfront. Sarıyer is known for its fishing fleet, while at Kilyos (a short bus ride away) you can swim in the Black Sea. Before returning to Istanbul, the ferry ties up for three hours at Anadolu Kavağı, giving you time to climb the hill to the Genoese castle, or lunch in a waterfront restaurant. If you return on the later ferry there's the bonus of a beautiful sunset as you approach the city.

THE BASICS

🚇 Departures from Eminönü: F8

🕐 Departures at 10.35 daily; also at noon and 1.35 mid-Jun to mid-Sep

🍽 Fish restaurants at Sarıyer and Anadolu Kavağı

🚢 Eminönü, Beşiktaş, Kanlıca, Yeniköy, Sarıyer, Anadolu Kavağı

♿ None

💰 Expensive

HIGHLIGHTS

● Dolmabahçe Sarayı (▷ 96)
● Ortaköy Camii (▷ 101)
● Beylerbeyi Sarayı (▷ 94)
● Küçüksu Kasrı (▷ 100)
● Rumeli Hisarı (▷ 101)
● Anadolu Kavağı (▷ 99)
● Wooden mansions (_yalıs_)
● Kanlıca yoghurt

Dolmabahçe Sarayı

TOP 25

HIGHLIGHTS

- Marble façade
- Throne Room
- Ceremonial staircase
- Sultan's bathroom
- Atatürk's bedroom
- Clock stopped at exact time of Atatürk's death

TIP

- To see more palace treasures, visit the Depo Müze (Depot Museum), a vast Ottoman junk shop in the former palace kitchens at Beşiktaş.

Although the taste of the builders of Dolmabahçe Palace might be subject to doubt, the building's entertainment value lies in the sheer extravagance of its interiors—a relentless accumulation of ostentatious luxury and rococo excess.

A new palace By far the most sumptuous of the sultans' palaces, Dolmabahçe stands on the site of a reclaimed port—the Turkish word means 'filled-in garden'. It was commissioned by Sultan Abdülmecit from the architects Karabet Balyan and his son, Nikoğos, in 1843, and the royal entourage moved here from Topkapı 13 years later. The palace was so expensive, it contributed in part to the bankrupting of the Ottoman treasury in 1881. The first President of the Republic, Mustafa Kemal

It's certainly not plain—the sumptuous Dolmabahçe Palace helped to bankrupt the Ottoman treasury in 1881

Atatürk, stayed in Dolmabahçe in 1927, rechristening it the Palace of the Nation. He died here on 10 November 1938 during a visit.

Interiors The layout preserves the traditional division between *selamlık* (state rooms) and *harem* (private apartments). Separating the two is the largest throne room in the world, its trompe-l'oeil ceiling supported by 56 Corinthian columns. It was here that the first Ottoman parliament was convened in 1877. Other highlights include the magnificent formal staircase, with a balustrade of Baccarat crystal and the Hünkar Hamamı (Sultan's Bathroom), with walls of alabaster imported from Egypt. The decoration is almost exclusively Western, after a style the French novelist, Théophile Gautier, described ironically as 'Louis XIV *orientalisé*'.

THE BASICS

✚ Off map to northeast
✉ Dolmabahçe Caddesi, Beşiktaş
☎ 212-236-9000
🕐 May–end Oct Tue, Wed, Fri–Sun 9–4; Nov–end Apr Tue, Wed, Fri–Sun 9–3
🚌 Kabataş
♿ None
💷 Expensive (extra charge for photography)
❓ Allow 2 hours for a visit; guided tours only

Yıldız Parkı

Yıldız Şale (left) and
the Grand Room
(middle); a bandstand
in the park (right)

THE BASICS

➕ Off map to northeast
✉ Çırağan Caddesi,
between Beşiktaş and
Ortaköy
☎ Yıldız Şale: 212-259-
4570
🕐 Park: daily 9–6.
Yıldız Şale: Tue, Wed,
Fri–Sun 9.30–5 in summer,
9.30–4 in winter
🍴 Cafés (€) and Malta
Kiosk (€€€)
🚌 Beşiktaş
♿ None
💷 Park: free.
Yıldız Şale: inexpensive
❓ Yıldız Şale guided
tours only

HIGHLIGHTS

Park
● Malta Kiosk
● Yıldız Porcelain Factory
● Shady parks and gardens
Yıldız Şale
● Ceremonial Hall
● Hereke carpet (400sq m/
478sq yards)
● Banqueting Room

**The last of the great Ottoman palaces,
Yıldız Şarayı, is mainly popular for its
stunning grounds, Yıldız Park.**

Yıldız Parkı In a city with so much traffic and
noise, green space is at a premium and when
the people of Istanbul need to breathe, they
come to Yıldız Park. On weekend afternoons,
families picnic and lovers stroll in this magnificent 50ha (123-acre) park, scented with orange
blossom, on a wooded hillside above the
Bosphorus. The park was used as an
imperial estate in the reign of Sultan Ahmet
(1603–17), though the pavilions and kiosks
date from the late 19th century. Among the
buildings here are the Çadir Kiosk, now a
pleasant lakeside café; Malta Kiosk, a smart
restaurant with a terrace overlooking the river;
and Yıldız Porcelain Factory (▷ 104), built to
provide china for the palace kitchens and still
in use today.

Yilziz Şale Sultan Abdülhamid II commissioned the hilltop palace in 1875 because it
was thought to be more secure from attack
than Dolmabahçe (▷ 96–97). It turned out to
be the last of the Ottoman palaces to be built
in Istanbul. In addition to the palace, Yıldız
Şale, at the top of the park, was originally built
as a guesthouse to accommodate royal visitors
to the palace, but later became the sultan's
chief residence. Designed to resemble a Swiss
chalet, its 64 rooms contain an intriguing blend
of baroque and Islamic styles.

More to See

ANADOLU HISARI

This castle, on the Asian shore of the Bosphorus beneath Fatih Bridge, was begun in 1390 by Sultan Beyazıt I. The barbican and towers were added by Mehmet II just before the city's conquest in 1453. The 'Fortress of Anatolia' is closed to visitors, but it is impressive from the outside and is only a short walk from Küçüksu Kasrı (▷ 100).

⊞ Off map to northeast ⊠ Körfez Caddesi, Kanlıca 🍴 Café (€) nearby 🚌 15 from Üsküdar

ANADOLU KAVAĞI

The final stop on the Bosphorus ferry is a busy Asian fishing village, with restaurants by the port catering for the large number of day-trippers. A steep climb out of the village leads to Yoros Castle, a ruined Genoese fortress of Byzantine origin, whose clifftop setting offers outstanding views of the Bosphorus and Black Sea.

⊞ Off map to northeast 🍴 Lots of restaurants (€–€€€) 🚢 Anadolu Kavağı

BEŞIKTAŞ

Shortly after passing the white marble façade of Dolmabahçe Palace, the Bosphorus ferry makes its first stop, at Beşiktaş. You can watch the passengers disembark at the elegant art nouveau jetty, sip tea in waterside cafés, stroll along the promenade or visit the Deniz Müzesi (Naval Museum).

⊞ Off map to northeast ⊙ Naval Museum: Wed–Sun 9–5 🍴 Cafés (€) and restaurants (€€) 🚢 Beşiktaş

BÜYÜK ÇAMLICA

Climb 'Great Pine Mountain' at the highest point of the city (268m/879ft) to look over the Golden Horn and Sea of Marmara.

⊞ Off map to east ⊠ Büyükçamlıca Tepesi 🍴 Café and teahouse 🚢 Üsküdar, then taxi ✋ Free

ÇIRAĞAN SARAYI

This stately waterfront palace was commissioned by Sultan Abdülaziz and completed in 1874. His successor, Murat V, was confined here for

★

Ferries moored at the quayside at Beşiktaş

Climb to Yoros Castle, at Anadolu Kavağı, for great views

more than 30 years after he was deposed in 1876. The palace was destroyed by fire in 1910 and has been restored and reopened as a luxury hotel (▷ 112).

🕂 Off map to northeast ✉ Çırağan Caddesi 32, Beşiktaş ☎ 212-326-4646 🚢 Beşiktaş

ISTANBUL OYUNCAK MÜZESI

www.istanbuloyuncakmuzesi.com

Founded in 2005 by poet Sunay Akın in a wooden mansion, the Istanbul Toy Museum has a charming collection of antique toys. Puppet and magic shows are held here at weekends.

🕂 Off map to southeast ✉ Ömerpaşa Caddesi Dr Zeki Zeren Sokak 17, Göztepe ☎ 216-359-4550 🕐 Tue–Fri 9.30–6, Sat, Sun 9.30–7 🍴 Café (€) 🚌 Bus from Kadıköy to Göztepe 🚉 Göztepe 🎟 Moderate

KADIKÖY

Regular ferries from Eminönü take foot passengers to this busy shopping area on the Asian side, on the site of the ancient Greek city of Chalcedon. On the way there are magnificent views.

🕂 Off map to southeast 🚢 Kadıköy

KIZ KULESI

The 18th-century Kız Kulesi (Maiden's Tower) is on an island at the entrance to the Bosphorus. You can take a boat trip to the tower, which now houses a café. To get there, take the ferry to Üsküdar or Harem and follow the seaside promenade to the jetty at Salacak.

🕂 Off map to east ☎ 216-342-4747 🕐 Mon–Fri 12–7, Sat, Sun 11–7 🍴 Café and restaurant (€€) 🎟 Boat trip: moderate 🚢 Üsküdar

KÜÇÜKSU KASRI

This pleasing pseudo-baroque palace was built for Sultan Abdülmecit by Nikoğos Balyan in 1856–57. You can make the small tour of the palace or take a picnic in the meadows. In the gardens is a riverside boardwalk café and the delightful Küçüksu Fountain.

The Maiden's Tower guards the entrance to the Bosphorus

Ortaköy Camii, near Atatürk Bridge

🚻 Off map to northeast ✉ Küçüksu Caddesi ☎ 216-332-3303 🕐 Summer Tue, Wed, Fri–Sun 9.30–5; winter Tue, Wed, Fri–Sun 9.30–4 🚌 15 from Üsküdar ♿ None 💷 Inexpensive

ORTAKÖY

With the beautiful Ortaköy Camii reflected in the Bosphorus under the mighty Atatürk Bridge, Ortaköy is one of the most attractive spots in Istanbul. The square by the port is lined with fish restaurants; on Sunday morning the lanes come alive with an arts and crafts market.

🚻 Off map to northeast 🍴 Cafés (€) and restaurants (€€) 🚌 25E, 40 ⛴ Ortaköy

RUMELI HISARI

This superb fortress was built in 1452 by Mehmet II. You can explore the walls and garden terraces, and, in summer, attend a concert at the open-air arena.

🚻 Off map to northeast ✉ Yahya Kemal Caddesi 42, Rumeli Hisarı ☎ 212-263-5305 🕐 Thu–Tue 9.30–4 🚌 25E, 40 ♿ None 💷 Inexpensive

SADBERK HANIM MÜZESI

This private museum, a short walk south of the ferry dock at Sarıyer, has two wings. The first is devoted to archaeology, with items from Anatolian, Roman and Byzantine cultures, including oil lamps, glass jars and a clay goddess dating from 5000BC. The second section features Turkish arts, crafts and ethnography, with displays of Iznik tiles, embroidered costumes and a fascinating exhibition on marriage, childbirth and circumcision customs.

🚻 Off map to northeast ✉ Büyükdere Piyası Caddesi 27–29, Sarıyer ☎ 212-242-3813 🕐 Thu–Tue 10–5 🍴 Tea garden (€) 💷 Moderate ⛴ Sarıyer

ÜSKÜDAR

Ferries cross the Bosphorus from Eminönü to Üsküdar at approximately 20-minute intervals. As you step ashore, notice the elaborate fountain, built by Sultan Ahmet III in memory of his mother.

🚻 Off map to east ⛴ Üsküdar

The Ottoman-style façade of the Sadberk Hanim Museum

Rumeli Hisari was built by Mehmet II in four months for the siege of Constantinople

Excursions

THE BASICS

Distance: 30km
(18.5 miles)
Journey time: 1 hour
🚌 25E, 40 to Sarıyer, then
dolmuş or 151 to Kilyos;
150 to Rumeli Feneri
🚢 Sarıyer, then *dolmuş*
or bus

KILYOS

The seaside resort of Kilyos lies on the European shores of the Black Sea. In former times this was little more than a fishing village, but it is now a major package holiday resort, with the nearest sandy beaches to Istanbul.

To get there, take a *dolmuş* from Sarıyer, and enjoy superb views of the Bosphorus and the Black Sea as the road winds over the hills. Unfortunately, access to the best beaches at Kilyos is possible only via private beach clubs such as Nonstop Beach and Solar Beach, whose daily admission charge includes the use of sun loungers and umbrellas. For a slightly more exclusive atmosphere, take a taxi or local bus from Sarıyer to the Golden Beach Club at Rumeli Feneri, with its lighthouse and Ottoman fortress guarding the entrance to the Bosphorus.

THE BASICS

Distance: 20km
(12.5 miles)
Journey time: 1–1.5
hours
🕐 Several departures
daily in summer, including
8.30am and 10am; fewer
in winter
🚢 From Kabataş
❓ Arrive at least 30 mins
before departure time
in summer

KIZIL ADALAR (PRINCES' ISLANDS)

This archipelago off the Asian coast of the Sea of Marmara is Istanbul's most popular resort, and the ferries are crowded on summer weekends with day-trippers and picnicking families.

The ferry from Kabataş calls at four separate islands—Kınalıada, Burguzada, Heybeliada and Büyükada (pictured right). If you just want to chill out on a beach, Kınalıada is a 50-minute ride from Istanbul and there is a large pebble beach right by the port. The larger islands have sandy coves and clifftop walks, as well as the steep climb to St. George's Monastery on Büyükada. Motor traffic is prohibited on the islands so there are no taxis, but you can rent a bicycle to get around or take a horse-and-trap ride on Heybeliada or Büyükada.

Shopping

AKMERKEZ
The biggest and best of the American-style shopping malls springing up in the city, this has chains such as Benetton and Zara, designer clothes from Vakko, plus jewellers, book and music stores, a cinema and restaurants. To get there, take the metro from Taksim Square.
➕ Off map ✉ Nispetiye Caddesi, Etiler ☎ 212-282-0170 🔲 Levent

KANYON
www.kanyon.com.tr
Opened in 2006, Istanbul's newest

shopping mall has won architectural awards for its design, with open-air corridors around a dramatic interior canyon. There is a flagship branch of Harvey Nichols, together with local and global fashion brands, cinemas and restaurants.
➕ Off map ✉ Büyükdere Caddesi 185, Levent ☎ 212-353-5300 🕙 Daily 10–10 🔲 Levent

TIFFANY COLLECTION
Shop in the luxurious surroundings of the shopping arcade at the

Çirağan Palace hotel (▷ 112), which includes a jewellery showroom featuring exclusive Tiffany products.
➕ Off map ✉ Çirağan Caddesi 32, Beşiktaş ☎ 212-259-8795 🚇 Beşiktaş

YILDIZ PORSELEN FABRIKASI
Just beside the entrance to the red-brick factory, in the grounds of Yıldız Park (▷ 98), is a small shop selling famous home-produced porcelain.
➕ Off map ✉ Yıldız Parkı ☎ 212-260-2370

Entertainment and Nightlife

REINA
Famous summertime megaclub on the banks of the Bosphorus, where Istanbul's celebrities and wannabes hang out on balmy nights.
➕ Off map ✉ Muallim Naci Caddesi, Ortaköy ☎ 212-259-5919 🕙 Jun–end Sep daily 7pm–4am

SOCCER
Most male Turks are passionate about soccer and the three biggest teams (Beşiktaş, Fenerbahçe and Galatasaray) all play in Istanbul. Beşiktaş play at the İnönü stadium,

close to Dolmabahçe Palace; Galatasaray at the Ali Sami Yen stadium in the north of the city; and Fenerbahçe at

TURKISH GRAND PRIX

Istanbul became a new name on the Formula One circuit in 2005 when it hosted the Turkish Grand Prix at the Istanbul Park race track in Tuzla, close to Sabiha Gökçen Airport, in front of a sell-out crowd of 125,000 spectators. The Turkish Grand Prix is now an established event on the calendar.

the Şükrü Saracoğlu stadium in Kadıköy, which will host the 2009 UEFA Cup final. Most league matches take place on weekends from August to May, with European fixtures midweek. Tickets go on sale a few days beforehand, at the stadiums and at Biletix outlets.
Beşiktaş: www.bjk.com.tr ☎ 212-310-1000
Fenerbahçe: www.fenerbahce.org ☎ 216-542-1907
Galatasaray: www.galatasaray.org ☎ 212-216-1500

Restaurants

PRICES

Prices are approximate, based on a three-course meal for one person.

€€€	more than 40 YTL
€€	20–40 YTL
€	under 20 YTL

ALI BABA (€€€)

One of the best waterfront fish restaurants awaits passengers arriving on the ferry at Büyükada.

✚ Off map ✉ Gülistan Caddesi 18, Büyükada ☎ 216-382-3733 🕐 Summer daily 12–12; winter daily 12–6 ⛴ Büyükada, Princes' Islands

AQUARIUS (€€€)

This well-known fish restaurant beside the port at Sarıyer has three floors of seating and an extensive riverside terrace.

✚ Off map ✉ Balıkçılar Çarşısı, Sarıyer ☎ 212-271-3434 🕐 Daily 12–12 ⛴ Sarıyer

ASIRLIK KANLICA YOĞURDU (€)

The village of Kanlıca is famous for its yoghurt (▷ 95), which you can sample at this waterfront café beside the Bosphorus. Alternatively stay on the ferry to Anadolu Kavağı and pots of yoghurt will be brought on board.

✚ Off map ✉ Iskele Yanı 2, Kanlıca ☎ 216-413-4469 🕐 Daily 9–9 ⛴ Kanlıca

AYA YORGI MANASTIRI (€)

Grilled meat on an outdoor terrace with fabulous views beside St. George's Monastery —a good place to relax after the steep climb.

✚ Off map ✉ Aya Yorgi Manastırı, Büyükada ☎ No phone 🕐 Daily noon–9pm ⛴ Büyükada, Princes' Islands

BABA (€€)

Turn left on leaving the ferry at Anadolu Kavağı and walk to the end of the village to reach this attractive fish restaurant, with a terrace right over the water.

✚ Off map ✉ Iskele Caddesi 13, Anadolu Kavağı ☎ 216-320-2047 🕐 Daily 12–12 ⛴ Anadolu Kavağı

BANYAN (€€€)

Stylish Southeast Asian fusion food in a stunning waterfront setting beside the Bosphorus at Ortaköy. Try the Banyan plate for two to share, which includes crispy vegetables, prawns, sushi and spicy dips, followed by lamb satay or steak with teriyaki and almond mash.

✚ Off map ✉ Muallim Naci Caddesi, Salhane Sokak 3, Ortaköy ☎ 212-259-9060 🕐 Mon–Sat 12–12, Sun 10am–midnight ⛴ Ortaköy

CENEVIZ CAFÉ (€)

Simple dishes of mackerel, bread and salad served at outdoor tables on the square in front of the ferry terminus at Anadolu Kavağı.

✚ Off map ✉ Iskele Meydanı, Anadolu Kavağı ☎ 216-320-2058 🕐 Daily 12–12 ⛴ Anadolu Kavağı

ÇINAR (€€)

Waterfront restaurant with outdoor tables on the square by the port at Ortaköy, with a wide choice of *mezes* and fresh fish.

✚ Off map ✉ Iskele Meydanı, Ortaköy ☎ 212-261-5818 🕐 Daily noon–1am ⛴ Ortaköy

CLEMENT'S (€€€)

Smart restaurant in an old Bosphorus mansion at Yeniköy, which once belonged to the Ottoman vizier Sait Halim Paşa.

✚ Off map ✉ Köybası Caddesi 117, Yeniköy ☎ 212-223-0566 🕐 Daily 8pm–2am ⛴ Yeniköy

ORTAKÖY DINING

Ortaköy, one of Istanbul's most vibrant districts, has a waterfront lined with cafés and terrace restaurants that boast superb views of the Bosphorus, as well as of the exquisite 19th-century Ortaköy Mosque. A street market draws the crowds on Sunday, and there are also craft and junk shops to explore.

105

DENIZ KIZI (€€)

Intimate, cosy little fish restaurant near the port at Sarıyer, with a handful of outdoor tables under a shady terrace.

⊞ Off map ⊠ Balıkçılar Çarşısı, Sarıyer ☎ 212-242-8570 ⏰ Daily 12–12 🚢 Sarıyer

KANAAT (€)

Founded in 1933, this large no-frills *lokanta*, a short walk from the ferry dock, serves dishes such as vegetables in olive oil and cucumber with yoghurt, as well as homemade desserts.

⊞ Off map ⊠ Selmanı Pak Caddesi 25, Üsküdar ☎ 216-341-5444 ⏰ Daily 9am–11pm 🚢 Üsküdar

KAVAK DOĞANAY (€€)

The oldest of the fish restaurants in Anadolu Kavağı is in a perfect setting by the port with a waterfront terrace.

⊞ Off map ⊠ Yalı Caddesi 13, Anadolu Kavağı ☎ 216-320-2036 ⏰ Daily 12–12 🚢 Anadolu Kavağı

KÖRFEZ (€€€)

A smart waterfront restaurant with a summer garden on the Asian shore of the Bosphorus at Kanlıca, Körfez is reputed to serve some of the best fish in Istanbul, including the house special, sea bass baked in salt. Reserve ahead and you can be picked up by the restaurant's private boat, which is moored at Rumeli Hisarı on the European shore.

⊞ Off map ⊠ Körfez Caddesi 78, Kanlıca ☎ 216-413-4314 ⏰ Daily 12–12 🚢 Kanlıca

RUMELI ISKELE (€€)

Enjoy tasty seafood *mezes* and fish dishes in this popular restaurant near the fortress at Rumeli Hisarı, with views across the water to Anadolu Hisarı on the far side.

⊞ Off map ⊠ Yahya Kemal Caddesi 1, Rumeli Hisarı ☎ 212-263-2997 ⏰ Daily 12–12 🚌 25E or 40 to Rumeli Hisarı

VOGUE (€€€)

Hang out with the beautiful people at this ultra-trendy Beşiktaş restaurant, with a 13th-floor rooftop terrace overlooking the Bosphorus, and a menu that ranges in style from sushi to Turkish-Mediterranean fusion dishes.

⊞ Off map ⊠ Spor Caddesi 92, Beşiktaş ☎ 212-227-4404 ⏰ Daily 12–3, 7pm–2am 🚢 Beşiktaş

YELKEN (€€€)

This pretty waterfront restaurant beside the ferry dock at Yeniköy features fish dishes such as stuffed sea bass, paella and seafood spaghetti. In summer, you can eat on a terrace above the water.

⊞ Off map ⊠ Köybası Caddesi 109, Yeniköy ☎ 212-262-9490 ⏰ Daily 12–12 🚢 Yeniköy

YOROS CAFÉ (€€)

Occupying a series of terraces tumbling down the hillside beneath Yoros Castle, this open-air restaurant serves a simple menu of grilled fish, mussels, chips and salad, with the bonus of some magnificent views over the Bosphorus. It offers a bargain fixed-price lunch menu of mackerel, squid, mussels, salad and drinks.

⊞ Off map ⊠ Baba Sokak 76, Anadolu Kavağı ☎ 216-320-2028 ⏰ Daily 12–12 🚢 Anadolu Kavağı

FISHERMAN'S CATCH

Balık—fish
Hamsi—anchovy
Istavrit—mackerel
Kalamar—squid
Karides—prawns
Kılıç—swordfish
Levrek—bass
Lüfer—blue fish
Midye—mussels
Palamut/torik—bonito
Tekir—mullet
Yengeç—crab

Istanbul has accommodation for all styles and budgets, from inexpensive hostels to five-star hotels. If you want a room with character, stay in a restored Ottoman-era house in Sultanahmet or sleep in a sultan's palace on the Bosphorus shore.

Where to Stay

Introduction

The range of accommodation options is growing all the time, with new apartments, waterfront mansions and boutique hotels. Rooms are at a premium during the summer, so reserve well in advance.

Districts

Most of the budget accommodation is in and around Sultanahmet. There are inexpensive hotels and backpacker hostels on Akbıyık Caddesi. This area also has a large number of 'Ottoman' hotels, in historic wooden houses with roof terraces overlooking the Sea of Marmara. The largest concentration of Ottoman hotels is in the quiet streets around Küçük Ayasofya. Most luxury accommodation is found north of the Golden Horn, in the area around Harbiye and Taksim Square. A recent trend has been the opening of chic boutique hotels in restored wooden mansions along the Bosphorus.

Practicalities

The peak season is from May to September, and you should reserve ahead at this time. Istanbul Hotels (www.istanbulhotels.com) has lists of hotels by area and includes links to the hotels' own websites. Prices are usually quoted in euros, though you can pay in Turkish lira. Most hotels accept credit cards but there may be a discount for paying in cash. The price of a room generally includes a full Turkish breakfast, with pastries, bread, cheese, eggs, olives and tomatoes.

HOTEL CHAINS

The big international hotel chains have branches in Istanbul. Try the Hilton (☎ 212-315-6000; www.hilton.com), Hyatt Regency (☎ 212-368-1234; www.istanbul.regency.hyatt.com), Mövenpick (☎ 212-319-2929; www.movenpick-hotels.com), Ritz-Carlton (☎ 212-334-4444; www.ritzcarlton.com) and Swissôtel (☎ 212-326-1100; www.swissotel.com). For longer stays, you could rent an apartment through Istanbul Rentals (☎ 212-638-7606; www.istanbulrentals.com).

Budget Hotels

Expect to pay between €30 and €60 per night for a double room in a budget hotel.

ANTIQUE

www.hotelantique.com
Antique is a small, friendly hotel with 17 simply furnished but comfortable rooms on a quiet street near the Arasta Bazaar. In summer, you can take your breakfast on the rooftop terrace.

⊞ G12 ⊠ Oğul Sokağı 17, Sultanahmet ☎ 212-516-4936 🚇 Sultanahmet

DENIZ KONAK

www.denizkonakhotel.com
Opened in 2006 by the owners of Sultan's Inn (▷ this page), the 'house of the sea' has 15 rooms in a newly restored wooden house in Küçük Ayasofya.

⊞ H12 ⊠ Çayiroğlu Sokağı 14, Sultanahmet ☎ 212-518-9595 🚇 Sultanahmet

HANEDAN

www.hanedanhotel.com
If you want to enjoy Ottoman style on a budget, try this small hotel in the heart of the Sultanahmet hotel district. It has 10 rooms, which are tastefully decorated with pale yellow walls, and its rooftop breakfast terrace gives you fabulous views.

⊞ H11 ⊠ Adliye Sokağı 3, Sultanahmet ☎ 212-516-4869 🚇 Sultanahmet

ORIENT HOSTEL

www.orienthostel.com
This hostel, with 92 beds in single and twin rooms and dorms, is at the heart of the back-packer scene, with belly-dancing, hookah and movie nights, a travel agency and inexpensive internet access for guests.

⊞ H11 ⊠ Akbıyık Caddesi 13, Sultanahmet ☎ 212-517-9493 🚇 Sultanahmet

PENINSULA

www.hotelpeninsula.com
On the same quiet street as the Hanedan (▷ this page), this small hotel in a restored

ROOM WITH A VIEW

If you're on a budget and can't afford to stay in a first-class hotel, you should still be able to find a 'room with a view' in İstanbul. Most of the lower-price hotels in Sultanahmet have a rooftop breakfast terrace or bar. Other extras that may be included are free internet access and a transfer from the airport—remember to ask about this when you book. You can sometimes get a discount by paying in cash, especially if you pay in euros or US dollars.

cream-painted town house, has 11 rooms and a penthouse suite, plus a roof terrace where you can lie on a hammock enjoying dreamy views of the Blue Mosque and the Sea of Marmara.

⊞ H11 ⊠ Adliye Sokağı 6, Sultanahmet ☎ 212-458-6850 🚇 Sultanahmet

SIDE HOTEL AND PENSION

www.sidehotel.com
One of the best options for those on a budget, this large establishment in Sultanahmet has a wide range of accommodation, from en suite hotel rooms to pension rooms with shared bathrooms, and family apartments.

⊞ G11 ⊠ Utangaç Sokağı 20, Sultanahmet ☎ 212-517-2282 🚇 Sultanahmet

SULTAN'S INN

www.sultansinn.com
An Ottoman-style hotel but in the budget category, this pretty mustard-painted town house in the Küçük Ayasofya district has stone walls, warm Anatolian fabrics and the obligatory roof terrace.

⊞ F12 ⊠ Mustafa Paşa Sokağı 50, Sultanahmet ☎ 212-638-2562 🚇 Sultanahmet

Mid-Range Hotels

Expect to pay between €60 and €120 per night for a double room in a mid-range hotel.

AMISOS

www.amisoshotel.com
This boutique hotel opposite Gülhane Park has the feel of an Ottoman *harem*, with rooms decorated in blue, pink and black or sumptuous red velvet drapes. By contrast, the North Shield British-style pub is on the ground floor.
➕ G9 ✉ Ebusuud Caddesi 2, Gülhane ☎ 212-512-7050 🚇 Gülhane

ARARAT

www.ararathotel.com
Small (12 rooms), arty hotel with dark wooden floors, canopy beds and Byzantine-inspired murals. The rooftop bar has views over the Sea of Marmara.
➕ G11 ✉ Torun Sokağı 3, Sultanahmet ☎ 212-516-0411 🚇 Sultanahmet

ARTEFES

www.artefes.com
This striking Ottoman wooden house, with flower-filled window boxes, is hidden away in the backstreets of Küçük Ayasofya. On warm days, enjoy breakfast on the rooftop terrace.
➕ F12 ✉ Çayiroğlu Sokağı 25, Sultanahmet ☎ 212-516-5863 🚇 Sultanahmet

ASMALI KONAK

www.asmalikonakhotel.com
Opened in 2007 in a family-owned town house in Küçük Ayasofya, the 'house of the vine' has eight rooms, decorated in classical Turkish style with antiques.
➕ F12 ✉ Mustafa Paşa Sokağı 57, Sultanahmet ☎ 212-638-3534 🚇 Sultanahmet

AYASOFYA PENSIONS

www.ayasofyapensions.com
Istanbul's original Ottoman-style hotel consists of 63 rooms in a row of beautifully converted wooden

OTTOMAN CHIC

The first Ottoman-style hotels appeared in Istanbul in the 1980s, when the Turkish Touring and Automobile Club renovated buildings of historical and architectural importance, such as the Ayasofya Pensions (▷ this page). Now there are numerous private hotels in the Sultanahmet district, many in the brightly painted wooden houses that are typical of the area. They all offer variations on Ottoman chic, which combines traditional fabrics and furniture with modern comforts and design.

houses in pastel shades and decorated in period style. The hotel takes up a cobbled street between Ayasofya and Topkapı Palace.
➕ H10 ✉ Soğukçeşme Sokağı, Sultanahmet ☎ 212-513 3660 🚇 Gülhane

BÜYÜK LONDRA

www.londrahotel.net
Built in 1892 at the same time as the nearby Pera Palas (▷ 84), Büyük Londra has a similarly nostalgic feel, though the 54 rooms are much less luxurious.
➕ G3 ✉ Meşrutiyet Caddesi 117, Tepebaşı ☎ 212-245-0670 🚇 Funicular to Tünel

DERSAADET

www.dersaadethotel.com
Dersaadet is a restored 19th-century wooden mansion with 17 rooms, with old-style wooden furniture and parquet floors, and a breakfast terrace with views of the Blue Mosque.
➕ G12 ✉ Kapı Agasi Sokağı 5, Küçük Ayasofya, Sultanahmet ☎ 212-458-0760 🚇 Sultanahmet

EMPRESS ZOE

www.emzoe.com
Named after a legendary 11th-century Byzantine empress, this tastefully converted stone house is the classic Ottoman-style hotel, with stone walls,

wooden floors, a wrought-iron staircase, kilims and textiles and a 15th-century hammam in the garden. There are 22 rooms.

⊞ H11 ⊠ Adliye Sokağı 10, Sultanahmet ☎ 212-518-2504 🚊 Sultanahmet

IBRAHIM PAŞA

www.ibrahimpasha.com
This small boutique hotel with 16 rooms, in a stone town house, combines Ottoman features with modern designer touches, such as flat-screen TVs and wireless internet access. There's also a roof terrace with good views.

⊞ F11 ⊠ Terzihane Sokağı 5, Sultanahmet ☎ 212-518-0394 🚊 Sultanahmet

KARIYE

www.kariyeotel.com
Kariye is a tastefully converted Ottoman wooden house with Turkish carpets, parquet floor and prints of old Istanbul in its 26 rooms, as well as the excellent Asitane restaurant (▷ 74).

⊞ b5 ⊠ Kariye Camii Sokağı 18, Edirnekapı ☎ 212-534-8414 🚊 Edirnekapı

KYBELE

www.kybelehotel.com
This small hotel near the Hippodrome is quirky and bright, with antique lanterns hanging from every ceiling

and rooms that are filled with kilims and knick-knacks.

⊞ G10 ⊠ Yerebatan Caddesi 35, Sultanahmet ☎ 212-511-7766 🚊 Sultanahmet

NOMADE

www.hotelnomade.com
In a busy restaurant area at the foot of Divan Yolu (▷ 38), this trendy hotel, run by two sisters, has 16 rooms that are painted in bright modern hues, as well as a lovely roof terrace.

⊞ G10 ⊠ Ticarethane Sokağı 15, Sultanahmet ☎ 212-513-8172 🚊 Sultanahmet

---

NORTH OF THE GOLDEN HORN

If you want to stay in Beyoğlu, close to the shopping, restaurants and nightlife, there are two good hotels in restored 19th-century buildings. The Richmond Hotel (☎ 212-252-5460; www.richmond hotels.com.tr) is the only hotel on Istiklal Caddesi (▷ 80–81), while the Anemon Galata (☎ 212-293-2343; www.anemon hotels.com) is on Galata Square, near the Galata Tower (▷ 82–83). Both have rooftop bars with stunning views. Rooms at both hotels start at around €200 per night.

POEM

www.hotelpoem.com
A 19th-century Ottoman wooden mansion, Poem has been converted into a tasteful small hotel, with rooms named after Turkish poets. There is a roof garden and also a breakfast terrace shaded by walnut and fig trees.

⊞ H11 ⊠ Terbıyık Sokağı 12, Sultanahmet ☎ 212-638-9744 🚊 Sultanahmet

SARNIÇ

www.sarnichotel.com
This Dutch-run hotel is named after the magnificent fifth-century Byzantine cistern in the basement. The hotel has a rooftop restaurant with views of the Blue Mosque.

⊞ G12 ⊠ Küçük Ayasofya Caddesi 26, Sultanahmet ☎ 212-518 2323 🚊 Sultanahmet

SOKULLU PAŞA

www.sokullupasahotel.com
Sokullu Paşa, in a 16th-century pink clapboard house, is part of the Best Western chain. It has 37 rooms, decorated in traditional style, and excellent facilities, including a hammam.

⊞ F11 ⊠ Şehit Mehmet Paşa Sokağı 5, Sultanahmet ☎ 212-518-1790 🚊 Sultanahmet

Luxury Hotels

PRICES

Expect to pay more than €150 per night for a double room in the hotels on this page.

BENTLEY

www.bentley-hotel.com
With its minimalist decor and achingly hip design, the Bentley is Istanbul's first boutique hotel—just the place to stay for a shopping spree in the nearby fashion stores of Teşvikiye and Nişantaşı.
✚ Off map at J1
✉ Halaskargazi Caddesi 75, Harbiye ☎ 212-291-7730
🚇 Harbiye

ÇIRAĞAN PALACE KEMPINSKI

www.ciraganpalace.com
This 19th-century sultan's palace is now a five-star hotel with magnificent views across the Bosphorus and every conceivable luxury. Many of its 315 rooms and suites have sea views and most are in a modern annex.
✚ Off map at J4
✉ Çirağan Caddesi 32, Beşiktaş ☎ 212-326-4646
🚇 Beşiktaş

ERESIN CROWN

www.eresincrown.com.tr
The only five-star hotel in Küçük Ayasofya has a rooftop restaurant and an archaeological museum displaying Roman and Byzantine remains discovered during its construction.
✚ F12 ✉ Küçük Ayasofya Caddesi 40, Sultanahmet
☎ 212-638-4428
🚇 Sultanahmet

FOUR SEASONS

www.fourseasons.com/istanbul
In a former high-security prison in Sultanahmet, the Four Seasons is now the best address in town, with warm tones, an open courtyard and 65 luxury rooms in the old cells.
✚ H11 ✉ Tevkifhane Sokağı 1, Sultanahmet

PERA PALACE

Istanbul's most celebrated hotel opened in 1895 for passengers arriving in Constantinople after their 68-hour journey on the Orient Express train from Paris. The last word in luxury, the hotel acquired its aura of mystery and suspense after crime writer Agatha Christie stayed here while writing her novel *Murder on the Orient Express*. Other famous guests have included the spy Mata Hari, film star Greta Garbo and Turkish president Kemal Atatürk. Currently closed for renovation, the Pera Palace is due to reopen in 2008 and will hopefully have lost none of its period glamour.

☎ 212-638 8200
🚇 Sultanahmet

MARMARA

www.themarmarahotels.com
Huge skyscraper on Taksim Square, close to the shops, restaurants and nightlife of Beyoğlu, with 410 rooms and magnificent views of the Bosphorus and the Sea of Marmara from the rooftop bar.
✚ J2 ✉ Taksim Meydanı
☎ 212-251-4696 🚇 Taksim
🚇 Taksim

LES OTTOMANS

www.lesottomans.com
With suites starting at just under €1,000 per night, including butler service, private cinema and vinotherapy spa, Les Ottomans is the ultimate in decadence and chic. It opened in 2006 in a wooden mansion by the Bosphorus.
✚ Off map at J4
✉ Muallim Naci Caddesi 68, Kuruçeşme ☎ 212-359-1500
🚇 Ortaköy

YEŞIL EV

www.istanbulyesilev.com
The 'green house' is a restored 19th-century Ottoman wooden mansion between Ayasofya and the Blue Mosque, with 19 rooms decorated in period style and a beautiful garden with a fountain at the heart.
✚ G11 ✉ Kabasakal Caddesi 5, Sultanahmet
☎ 212-517-6785
🚇 Sultanahmet

This section gives you all the practical information you need to plan your visit and make the most of your time in Istanbul.

Need to Know

Planning Ahead

When to Go

Istanbul is busiest from May to September, when the weather is consistently warm and sunny. In July and August the city can become uncomfortably hot and crowded and many locals escape to the islands or coast. The most pleasant times to visit are in late spring and early autumn.

TIME

Istanbul is two hours ahead of London, seven hours ahead of New York and ten hours ahead of Los Angeles.

AVERAGE DAILY MAXIMUM TEMPERATURES

JAN	FEB	MAR	APR	MAY	JUN	JUL	AUG	SEP	OCT	NOV	DEC
47°F	48°F	52°F	62°F	70°F	79°F	82°F	82°F	77°F	67°F	59°F	52°F
8°C	9°C	11°C	17°C	21°C	26°C	28°C	28°C	25°C	19°C	15°C	11°C

Winter (Dec–Feb) is cold, wet and windy with grey skies. There is frequent rain and occasional sleet and snow.
Spring (Mar–May) is a delightful time, with mild weather, longer days and the start of the tourist season.
Summer (Jun–Aug) is hot and humid, though evenings by the Bosphorus can be pleasantly cool. There are also occasional thunderstorms.
Autumn (Sep–Nov) brings rain, though the sea is still warm enough to swim in September.

WHAT'S ON

April *International Film Festival*: New releases of Turkish and foreign films are shown.
National Sovereignty and Children's Day (23 April): Schoolchildren parade along Istiklal Caddesi.
May *International Theatre Festival*: This drama event is held in even-numbered years.
Fatih Day (29 May): Marching bands, parades and fireworks mark the Ottoman conquest of Constantinople by Mehmet the Conqueror in 1453.

June/July *International Music Festival*: Istanbul's biggest cultural event sees concerts and recitals at venues including Aya Irini church (▷ 38).
July *International Jazz Festival*: An offshoot of the International Music Festival (▷ above).
July/August *Starry Nights*: Open-air rock, pop and folk concerts are held in the magnificent setting of the Ottoman fortress at Rumeli Hisarı (▷ 101) and in the open-air arena at Harbiye.

October *Akbank Jazz Festival*: Traditional and modern jazz concerts are held at venues throughout the city.
Republic Day (29 October): Patriotic displays and fireworks mark the anniversary of the proclamation of the Turkish Republic in 1923.
November *Anniversary of Atatürk's Death* (10 November): A minute's silence is observed across the city at 9.05am, the exact time of Kemal Atatürk's death.

Useful Websites

www.istanbul.com
Snazzy interactive web portal with hotel and restaurant listings and a calendar of events.

www.istanbul.gov.tr
The official site of the Istanbul Governor's office features history, tourist sights, a photo gallery and a weather forecast.

www.ibb.gov.tr
The Istanbul Metropolitan Municipality site has maps, photos and practical advice.

www.gototurkey.co.uk/
www.tourismturkey.org
Official sites of the Turkish Tourist Office in the UK and US, with practical information.

www.kultur.gov.tr
Website of the Ministry of Culture and Tourism, with good background information on Turkish arts, crafts and traditions.

www.turkeytravelplanner.com
Personal site of writer and Turkey expert Tim Brosnahan, packed with travel advice and amusing anecdotes and tips.

www.timeoutistanbul.com
Online version of the monthly *Time Out* magazine, with the lowdown on the hottest restaurants, clubs and bars, as well as up-to-date listings of films, music and sports.

www.millisaraylar.gov.tr
Official site of the national palaces, including Dolmabahçe, Beylerbeyi and Yıldız Şale.

www.turkishdailynews.com.tr
Turkey's English-language newspaper.

www.kapalicarsi.org.tr
Listings of every shop in the Grand Bazaar.

GOOD TRAVEL SITES

www.fodors.com
A complete travel-planning site. Book air tickets, cars and rooms; research prices and weather; pose questions to fellow tourists; and find links to other sites.

www.thy.com
Turkish Airlines site, with online booking facility.

www.ido.com.tr
Schedules and fares for ferry and seabus services

CYBERCAFÉS

Café Turka
✉ Divan Yolu Caddesi 22/2
☎ 212-514-6551
🕐 Daily 9am–2am
💷 3YTL per hour

Utantik
✉ Alayköşkü Caddesi 2
☎ 212 511-2433
🕐 Daily 9am–midnight
💷 3YTL per hour

Robin Hood
✉ Yeni Carşi Caddesi 8/4
☎ 212-244-8959
🕐 Daily 9am–midnight
💷 3YTL per hour

Yağmur
✉ Şehbender Sokağı 18/2
☎ 212-292-3020
🕐 Daily 9am–11pm
💷 3YTL per hour

Getting There

INSURANCE

As Turkey does not have reciprocal health-care agreements with other countries it is essential that all visitors take out comprehensive medical and emergency insurance.

GETTING YOUR BEARINGS

Istanbul can be disorientating for first-time visitors, but really it is very simple. The main sights are in Sultanahmet, south of the Golden Horn on the European side and connected to Atatürk airport by the coast road along the Sea of Marmara. North of the Golden Horn but still in Europe, Beyoğlu is the shopping, entertainment and nightlife quarter. The Bosphorus strait, which links the Sea of Marmara to the Black Sea, separates European from Asian Turkey and effectively divides the city in two.

AIRPORTS

Istanbul's main airport, Atatürk International Airport (IST), is 13.5km (8 miles) west of the city and has regular flights to major European, American and Asian cities. Facilities for visitors include car rental, exchange bureaux, ATMs, post office, pharmacy and tourist information office.

30km (18.5 miles)
20km (12 miles)
10km (6 miles)
Istanbul
Atatürk International Airport
Sabiha Gökçen Airport

ARRIVING AT ATATÜRK INTERNATIONAL AIRPORT

The primary international airport is Atatürk International Airport (IST), ☎ 212-465-5555. Some hotels provide free taxi or minibus shuttle services if you are staying more than three nights, so ask about this when you book. Otherwise the most convenient way of reaching the city by public transport is on the Metro/Light Rail Transit in the direction of Aksaray. Change at Zeytinburnu station for the tram to Sultanahmet or Eminönü. The Metro station is on the lower ground floor of the airport. Both Metro and tram run every

10 minutes or so from 6am to midnight and a *jeton* (token) for each section of the journey costs around 1.30 YTL.

If you are staying north of the Golden Horn, the Havaş airport bus leaves every 30 minutes, from 4am to midnight, and costs 9 YTL for the 1-hour journey to Taksim Square.

A taxi from the airport to Sultanahmet or Beyoğlu will cost around €20 or 30 YTL.

ARRIVING AT SABIHA GÖKÇEN AIRPORT
Istanbul's second airport is around 26km (16 miles) east of Kadıköy on the Asian shore of the Bosphorus at Kurtköy. It mostly handles domestic and budget flights, including those operated by EasyJet from London Luton. To reach the heart of the city by public transport, take bus number E10, which has regular departures from the airport. It takes about an hour to reach Kadıköy, where you can catch a ferry to Eminönü. Havaş airport buses leave shortly after the arrival of incoming flights and cost 7 YTL to Kadıköy and 9.50 YTL to Taksim Square via the Bosphorus Bridge. A taxi to Sultanahmet or Beyoğlu will cost around €50 or 75 YTL.

ARRIVING BY BUS
Long-distance and international buses arrive at the *Otogar* (bus station), 10km (6 miles) west of the city. Some bus companies offer a free minibus transfer into the city. The Metro from Atatürk airport to Aksaray stops at the *Otogar*; change at Aksaray for a tram to Sultanahmet or Eminönü. Buses from Asian Turkey arrive at Harem, from where you can catch a ferry to Eminönü.

ARRIVING BY TRAIN
Trains from European destinations arrive at Sirkeci station (☎ 212-527-0050), with onward connections by bus, tram and ferry. Trains from Asian destinations arrive at Haydarpaşa station (☎ 212-336-0475), near Kadıköy, from where you can pick up a ferry to Eminönü.

ENTRY REQUIREMENTS
Citizens of the UK, US, Canada, Australia and some EU countries need a visa, which can be purchased on arrival and is valid for multiple entries to Turkey over a three-month period. The visa counter at Atatürk airport is left of passport control, and you should obtain your visa before joining the passport line. Fees must be paid in foreign currency. In 2007 the cost was $20 for US citizens, £10 for UK visitors and €10 for other EU countries. Citizens of New Zealand and some EU countries, including France, Germany and Greece, just require a valid passport. Regulations can change, so always check before you travel.

CUSTOMS
● Duty-free allowances: 200 cigarettes, 50 cigars, 200g tobacco, 5 litres of wine and spirits. Additional allowance: 400 cigarettes, 100 cigars, 500g tobacco if you buy from a Turkish duty-free shop on arrival.
● Valuables should be registered on your passport on entry.
● Keep proofs of purchase for expensive items.
● The export of antiquities is forbidden.

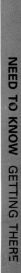

Getting Around

AKBIL TAG

One feature of the system that is useful for visitors is the Akbil tag, an electronic 'smart button' attached to a plastic holder, which contains credit for journeys. Akbil tags can be bought for a refundable deposit of 6 YTL at major bus and Metro terminals, including Aksaray, Eminönü, Sirkeci and Zeytinburnu. They can be charged with any amount of credit and used to pay for journeys by pressing the button into the electronic machine at turnstiles and on buses. Akbil fares are around 10 per cent lower than regular fares, so you save money as well as time queueing for tickets. Akbil tags are valid on buses, trams, the Metro, suburban trains, ferries, seabuses, the Tünel and Taksim funiculars, the Istiklal Caddesi tramway and the cable car from Eyüp to the Pierre Loti Café (▷ panel, 66).

Istanbul has a comprehensive and well integrated public transport network, including buses, trams, local trains, the Metro, funicular and ferries.

BUSES, TRAMS, TRAINS AND FUNICULAR

● The bus network is extensive, but travel is slow and vehicles are often crowded. Maps are displayed at bus stops and at major bus stations such as Eminönü and Taksim. The destination is shown on the front of the bus.

● Tickets can be bought at bus terminals and kiosks that display the sign '*IETT otobüs bileti*'. Drop the ticket into the box near the driver.

● The main tram route begins at Zeytinburnu and passes through Aksaray, Beyazıt, Çemberlitaş, Gülhane, Sirkeci and Eminönü before crossing the Galata Bridge to Karaköy and continuing via Tophane to Kabataş. Trams run every few minutes from 6am to midnight. *Jetons* are sold at kiosks beside the tram stops and must be fed into the turnstiles to enter the platform.

● Suburban trains from Sirkeci station follow the Marmara shore to Kumkapı, Yenikapı and Yedikule.

● The Tünel funicular railway, opened in 1875, connects the Karaköy end of Galata Bridge with Tünel Square, at the southern end of Istiklal Caddesi. Trains run every few minutes from 7am to 9pm.

● A modern funicular, opened in 2006, links the end of the tram line at Kabataş with the Metro station beneath Taksim Square.

● A vintage tram service runs along Istiklal Caddesi, linking Tünel with Taksim Square.

DOLMUŞES AND TAXIS

● The most common form of transport in Istanbul is the ubiquitous yellow taxi. Although taxis are more expensive than other means of transport, they are still relatively inexpensive and are easily the most convenient way to get around. All fares are

metered. Higher rates apply after midnight.

● *Dolmuşes* (shared taxis) are even cheaper. They follow assigned routes and stop on demand. Destinations are indicated on the windscreen (windshield). You are charged for the distance covered.

FERRIES

● Ferries ply up and down the Bosphorus and the Golden Horn.

● Timetables are posted outside the waiting room at ferry docks.

● Buy a *jeton* from the ticket window and drop it into the turnstile to enter the waiting area.

● When the boat is ready to leave, the doors will open for you to board. The main departure point is Eminönü, where jetties (*iskele*) serve the Golden Horn, Bosphorus (round-trip), Üsküdar, Kadıköy and Harem (car ferry). Ferries to the Princes' Islands depart from Kabataş. For timetables and routes, pick up a leaflet at Eminönü dock or call Ido (☎ 212-444-4436; www.ido.com.tr).

● Fast catamarans or seabuses (*deniz otobüsü*) ply busy commuter routes from Yenikapı and Kabataş.

METRO

● A short Metro commuter line heads north from Taksim to Levent, convenient for the Akmerkez and Metro City shopping malls.

● A second Metro commuter line connects Atatürk International Airport to Aksaray, 3km (2 miles) west of Sultanahmet. One of the stops is at the *Otogar* (Bus Station). The stations at Aksaray and Zeytinburnu are convenient interchanges for the tram line to Sultanahmet and Eminönü.

● Construction work is under way to extend both Metro lines to the seabus terminal at Yenikapı, linking them with eachother.

● *Jetons* for the Metro are sold at stations and must be fed into the turnstiles to enter the platform.

PLANNING AHEAD

Istanbul's public transport infrastructure is struggling to cope with the growing population and major investment is taking place. The Marmaray Project, begun in 2004, will create an uninterrupted 76km (48-mile) rail link from Halkali on the European side to Gebze in Asia. The highlight of the project is a tunnel beneath the Bosphorus from Sirkeci to Üsküdar. Construction work at Sirkeci and Üsküdar has unearthed Byzantine relics, which are now on display in the Archaeological Museum (▷ 24).

VISITORS WITH DISABILITIES

Istanbul is not an easy city for visitors with disabilities to negotiate. Streets are crowded and uneven, and few public buildings, toilets or transport facilities are wheelchair-accessible. There are plans to improve access to buses, trams and ferries, but for the time being provision for visitors with disabilities is limited.

Essential Facts

CONSULATES

● **Australia** ✉ Asker Ocaği Caddesi 15, Elmadağ ☎ 212-243-1333
● **Canada** ✉ Istiklal Caddesi 189, Beyoğlu ☎ 212-251-9838
● **Ireland** ✉ Ali Riza Gürcan Caddesi, Merter ☎ 212-482-1862
● **UK** ✉ Meşrutiyet Caddesi 34, Tepebaşı ☎ 212-334-6400
● **US** ✉ Kaplıcalar Mevkii 2, Istinye ☎ 212-335-9000

EMERGENCY PHONE NUMBERS

● Fire ☎ 110
● Ambulance ☎ 112
● Police ☎ 155
● Tourist Police ☎ 212-527-4503

ELECTRICITY

● 220 volts AC; two-pronged round-pin plugs are used.

ETIQUETTE

● Turkish people are generally friendly, polite and modest—you will earn their respect if you behave in the same way.
● When visiting mosques wear longer skirts or trousers and long-sleeved tops. Women should cover their heads.
● Always remove your shoes when you enter a mosque and a Turkish house or apartment.

MEDICAL TREATMENT

● There is no free health care for visitors, so make sure you have health insurance.
● For minor ailments, go to a pharmacy.
● Private hospitals: American Hospital ✉ Güzelbahçe Sokak, Nişantaşı ☎ 212-444-3777; Florence Nightingale Hospital ✉ Abidei Hürriyet Caddesi 290, Çağlayan Şişli ☎ 212-224-4950; International Hospital ✉ Istanbul Caddesi 82, Yeşilköy ☎ 212-663-3000.
● State hospital: Taksim Hastanesi (for emergency treatment only) ✉ Siraselviler Caddesi 112, Beyoğlu ☎ 212-252-4300.

MEDICINES

● Pharmacies sell imported drugs as well as local medicines.
● Pharmacists are qualified to take your blood pressure and administer first aid.
● Pharmacists have a 24-hour rota service: addresses are displayed in their windows.

OPENING HOURS

● Shops: Mon–Sat 9–7.
● Government offices: Mon–Fri 9–12.30, 1.30–5.
● Banks: Mon–Fri 9–12, 1.30–5.
● All are closed on public holidays and the first day(s) of religious holidays.

PLACES OF WORSHIP
● Mosques: There are more than 2,500 mosques in Istanbul.
● Greek Orthodox Patriarchate: ✉ Sadrazam Ali Paşa Caddesi, Fener ☎ 212-531-9670.
● Roman Catholic: St. Antony ✉ Istiklal Caddesi 325, Beyoğlu ☎ 212-244-0935.
● Protestant: German Church ✉ Emin Camii Sokağı 40, Beyoğlu ☎ 212-250-3040.
● Anglican: Christ Church ✉ Serdar-i Ekrem Sokağı 82 ☎ 212-251-5616.
● Synagogues: Neve Shalom ✉ Büyük Hendek Caddesi 61, Şişhane ☎ 212-293-6223; Askhenazi ✉ Yüksekkaldırım Caddesi, Karaköy ☎ 212-243-6909.

POSTAL SERVICE
● Stamps are sold from post offices and some shops selling postcards
● Post boxes are yellow, but you may find it more reliable to drop your letters off at a post office.
● PTT (Post-Telephone-Telegram) signs are written in black on a yellow background.
● The main post office is at Şehin Şah Pehlevi Caddesi, near Sirkeci station. Other post offices are in Galatasaray Meydanı in Beyoğlu and the Grand Bazaar.

SENSIBLE PRECAUTIONS
● Take sunglasses, a hat and sun-screen.
● Avoid raw foods and ice cubes.
● Tap water is officially safe to drink but it is heavily chlorinated. Bottled water is widely available.
● Watch your valuables in crowded locations and don't leave them in hotel rooms.
● Mugging, bag-snatching and other street crimes are not common in Istanbul, but avoid isolated areas at night.
● Do not get into a taxi that already has a passenger.
● Act with the same caution as you would in other cities.

LOST PROPERTY
Report lost passports to the Tourist Police
✉ Yerebatan Caddesi, Sultanahmet
☎ 212-527-4503

MONEY
The official currency is the New Turkish Lira (YTL), introduced in 2005. Notes are in denominations of 1, 5, 10, 20, 50 and 100 YTL and coins in denominations of 1, 5, 10, 25 and 50 kurus and 1 YTL. Euros (€) are also widely accepted. There are numerous ATMs across the city, which accept major credit and debit cards.

5 YTL

10 YTL

50 YTL

100 YTL

NATIONAL HOLIDAYS

● 1 Jan: New Year's Day
● 23 Apr: National Sovereignty and Children's Day
● 19 May: Youth and Sports Day
● 30 Aug: Victory Day
● 29 Oct: Republic Day
In addition to these, the major Islamic religious holidays (▷ below) are also national holidays.

RELIGIOUS HOLIDAYS

● The holy month of Ramadan, when Muslims fast between sunrise and sunset, lasts for four weeks before Şeker Bayramı.
● Şeker Bayramı (three days, dates vary).
● Kurban Bayramı (four days, dates vary).

TIPPING

It is usual to leave about 10 per cent of the bill as a tip (gratuity) in restaurants. Like everywhere else, taxi drivers appreciate a small tip, and you are also expected to tip masseurs and attendants at hammams (Turkish baths).

TELEPHONES

● Public telephone booths use a phonecard, which can be bought at post offices and kiosks in amounts of 50, 100 and 200 units.
● The code for Istanbul is 212 on the European side and 216 on the Asian side. To call a number on the same side of the Bosphorus, omit the prefix. For calls across the Bosphorus, dial 0 before the number, including the prefix.
● For international calls, dial 00, followed by the country code (US = 1, UK = 44) before the number.
● To call Istanbul from abroad, dial the international access code (US = 011, UK = 00), followed by 90, then the full number.
● International operator ☎ 115.
● Directory assistance ☎ 118.
● Most mobile phones will connect to local networks if you have arranged international roaming.

TOILETS

● There are toilets near mosques and in museums and cafés. It is customary to leave a small tip in the plate by the door.
● A few old-style toilets (two footholds and a hole in the ground) still exist in Istanbul.

TOURIST OFFICES

● Official guides can be booked through tourist information offices (▷ below).
● There are also plenty of unofficial guides willing to help. Agree on a price before you embark on a trip.
● The most useful office is in Sultanahmet, at the northeastern end of the Hippodrome ☎ 212-518-1802 🕐 Daily 9–5.
● There is a 24-hour tourist office in the arrivals hall at Atatürk International Airport, and tourist information counters for arriving passengers at Sirkeci station and Karaköy shipping terminal. There is also a tourist information office on Cumhuriyet Caddesi, in the arcade in front of the Istanbul Hilton.

Language

USEFUL PHRASES

hello	merhaba
goodbye	allaha ısmarladık (person going)
goodbye	güle güle (person staying)
yes	evet
no	hayır/yok
please	lütfen
thank you	teşekkür ederim/mersi
you're welcome	bir şey değil
I don't understand	sizi anlamiyorum
do you speak English?	Ingilizce biliyor musunuz?
open	açik
closed	kapalı
leave me alone	bırak beni

HOTELS

hotel	hotel/otel
bed and-breakfast	pansiyon
do you have a room?	boş odanız var mi?
single/double/triple	tek/çift/üç kişilik
I have a reservation	reservasyonım var
balcony	balkon
elevator	asansör
room service	oda servisi
air-conditioning	klima
hot water	sicak su
bath	banyo

RESTAURANTS

I'd like a table for two	Iki kişilik bir masa
menu	fiyat listesi
soup	çorba
fish	balık
meat/vegetarian dishes	etli/etsiz yemekler
red/white wine	kırmızı/beyaz şarap
bill	hesap
service included	servos dahilli

TRANSPORT

aeroplane	uçak
airport	havaalanı
train	tren
railway station	tren ıstasyonu
bus	otobus
bus stop	emanet
bus station	otogar
taxi	taksi
car	araba
petrol	benzin
boat	gemi
ferry	vapur/feribot
port	liman
ticket	bilet
single/return	gidiş/gidiş dönüş

MONEY

bank	banka
exchange office	döriz
post office	postane
travellers' cheque	seyahat çeki
credit card	kredi kartı
exchange rate	dövis kuru
how much?	ne kadar?
expensive	pahalı
what is the price?	fıatı nedir?
10	on
50	elli
100	yüz
200	ikiyüz
1,000	bin

Timeline

SÜLEYMAN THE MAGNIFICENT

The Ottoman empire reached its zenith under Süleyman I, whose 46-year reign, which began in 1520, made him the longest serving of all the sultans. Under his rule, Istanbul became the most powerful city in the world, with territories stretching from Cairo to Budapest. Süleyman fell in love with and married Roxelana, a beautiful Russian slave girl, refusing to take any other wives or concubines. The two of them are buried in the grounds of the Süleymaniye Mosque, the masterpiece of Süleyman's chief architect Mimar Sinan (▷ 54).

657BC The Greek colony of Byzantium is founded at Seraglio Point.

133BC Byzantium becomes part of the Roman province of Asia Minor.

AD330 Emperor Constantine decrees that Byzantium is to be the new capital of the Roman empire.

395 The Roman empire is officially divided into two, with Byzantium (now Constantinople) becoming the capital of the Eastern Roman empire.

412–22 Theodosius II orders the building of a new wall around the city.

527–65 Reign of Emperor Justinian. Ayasofya is built and the empire extends its influence from Spain to Iran.

1204 Constantinople is sacked during the Fourth Crusade.

1453 The city falls to Ottoman Sultan Mehmet II (the 'Conqueror') after a seven-week siege.

1461–65 The Topkapı Palace is built.

1520–66 Reign of Sultan Süleyman the Magnificent (▷ panel).

1617 Building of the Blue Mosque.

Left to right: Atatürk; the siege of Constantinople; Topkapı Palace; the Sultanahmet Camii, also known as the Blue Mosque; the Turkish flag

1856 Sultan Abdülmecit moves out of Topkapı Palace and into Dolmabahçe.

1883 The Orient Express first arrives in Istanbul.

1914 Following the Balkan Wars and the collapse of the Ottoman empire, Turkey enters World War I on Germany's side. Allied forces occupy Istanbul at the end of the war.

1922–23 After a three-year War of Independence, Mustafa Kemal Atatürk (▷ panel) proclaims the Turkish Republic, moving the capital from Istanbul to Ankara.

1938 Atatürk dies in Dolmabahçe Palace.

1939–45 Turkey remains neutral during World War II.

1994 Recep Erdoğan of the Islamic Welfare Party is elected mayor of Istanbul.

2003 More than 50 people die in bomb attacks on synagogues, the British consulate and HSBC bank.

2005 Istanbul hosts the Champions League soccer final and the first Turkish Grand Prix. Turkey begins entry talks with the European Union.

2010 Istanbul will be joint European Capital of Culture.

KEMAL ATATÜRK

Born in Salonika (Thessaloniki) in 1880, Mustafa Kemal became a national hero after defeating the Allied forces at Gallipoli in 1915. Following the collapse of the Ottoman empire and defeat in World War I, he led a war of independence, expelling all occupying forces from Turkey. As president of the Turkish Republic from 1923 until his death in 1938, he transformed the country, moving the capital to Ankara, abolishing the fez and other forms of religious dress, giving women the vote and introducing the Western calendar and Latin script in an effort to create a secular, European society In 1934 he adopted the surname Atatürk ('Father of the Turks'), and he is still revered throughout the country as the founding father of the nation.

THE FLAG OF THE REPUBLIC OF TURKEY

Index

INDEX

CITYPACK TOP 25
Istanbul

WRITTEN BY Christopher and Melanie Rice
ADDITIONAL WRITING Tony Kelly
DESIGN CONCEPT Kate Harling
COVER DESIGN AND DESIGN WORK Jacqueline Bailey
INDEXER Marie Lorimer
IMAGE RETOUCHING AND REPRO Michael Moody, Sarah Montgomery
EDITOR Kathryn Glendenning
SERIES EDITORS Paul Mitchell, Edith Summerhayes

First published 1997
Colour separation by Keenes, Andover
Printed and bound by Leo Paper Products, China

A CIP catalogue record for this book is available from the British Library.

ISBN 978-0-7495-5702-7

Published by AA Publishing, a trading name of Automobile Association Developments Limited, whose registered office is Fanum House, Basing View, Basingstoke, Hampshire RG21 4EA. Registered number 1878835.

A03145
Mapping in this title produced from mapping © MAIRDUMONT / Falk Verlag 2008
Transport map © Communicarta Ltd, UK